U2 THE BEST OF 1990-2000

ISBN 0-634-08638-3

HAL•LEONARD®
CORPORATION

7777 W. BLUEMOUND RD. P.O. BOX 13819 MILWAUKEE, WI 53213

Visit Hal Leonard Online at
www.halleonard.com

EVEN BETTER THAN THE REAL THING

Lyrics by BONO and THE EDGE
Music by U2

Moderate Rock

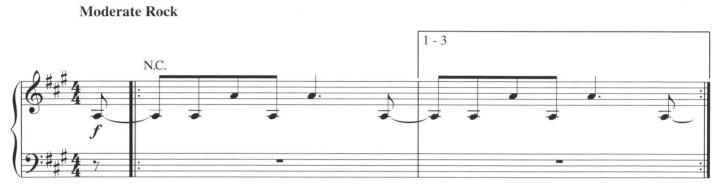

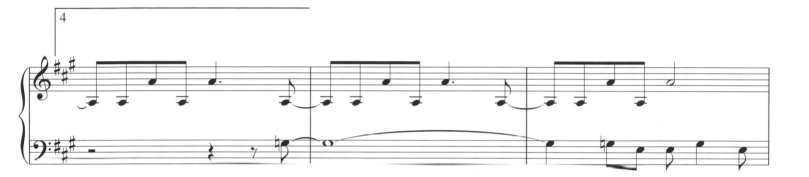

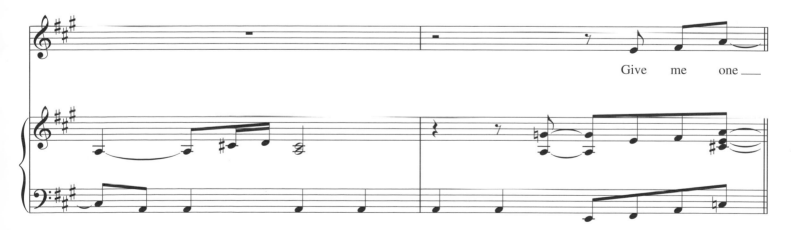

Give me one ___

more chance and you'll be sat - is - fied. _
last chance and I'm gon - na make you sing. _

Give me two _ more chanc - es.
Give me half _ a chance _ to

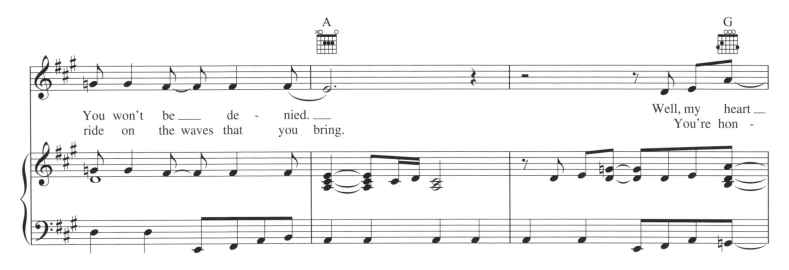

You won't be _ de - nied. _ Well, my heart
ride on the waves that you bring. You're hon -

_ is where it's al - ways been. _ My
- ey, child, to a swarm of bees. Gon - na

head is some-where in ___ be - tween. ___ Give me one ___
blow right through ___ you like ___ a breeze. ___ Give me one ___

___ more chance. Let ___ me be your lov - er to -
___ last chance. We'll slide down the sur - face of ___

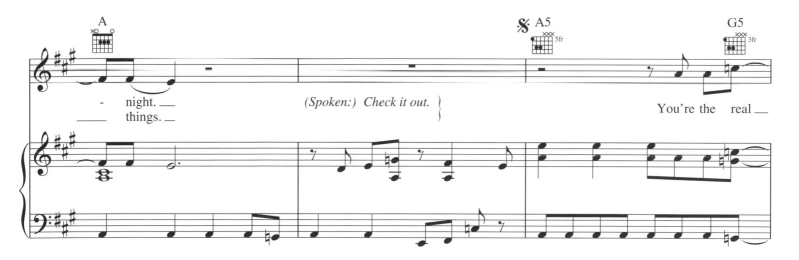

- night. ___ (Spoken:) Check it out. You're the real ___
___ things. ___

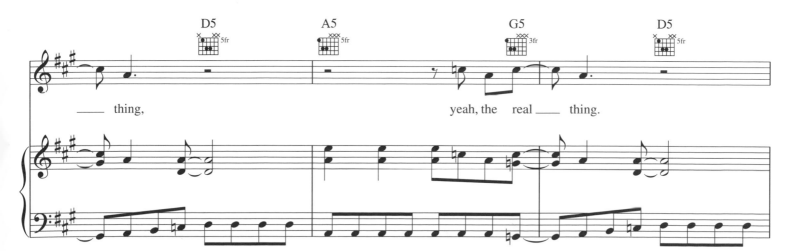

___ thing, yeah, the real ___ thing.

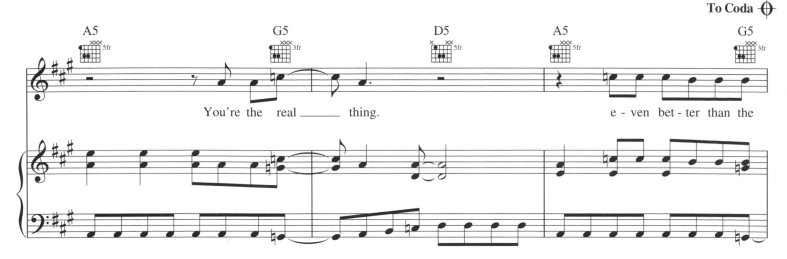

You're the real _____ thing. e - ven bet - ter than the

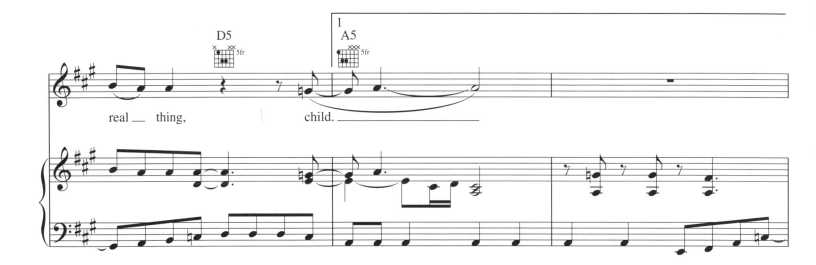

real __ thing, child. _____

Give me one __ _____

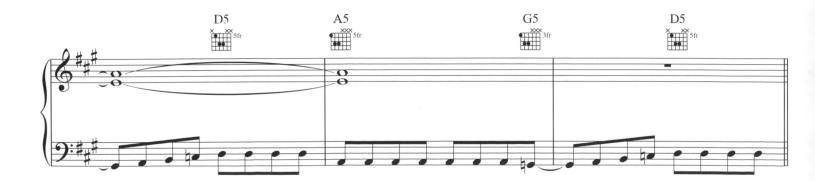

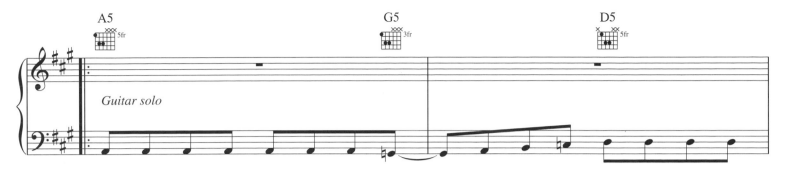

Guitar solo

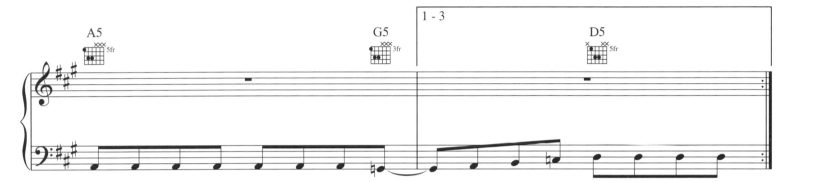

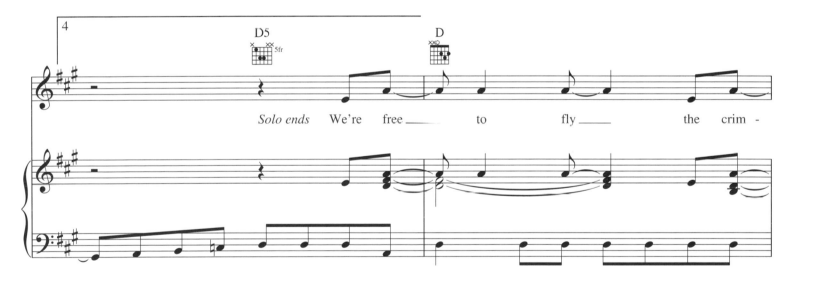

Solo ends We're free ___ to fly ___ the crim -

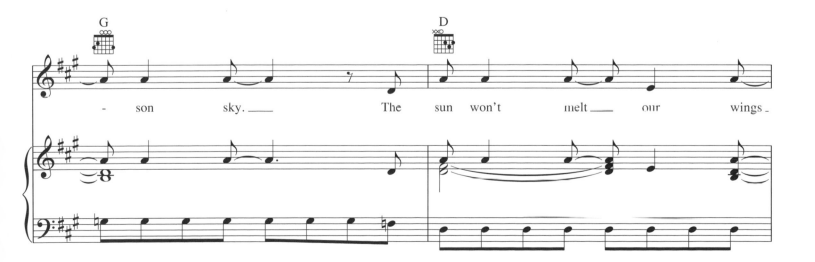

- son sky. ___ The sun won't melt ___ our wings ___

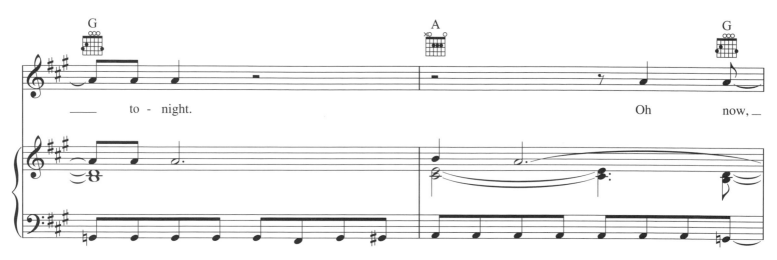

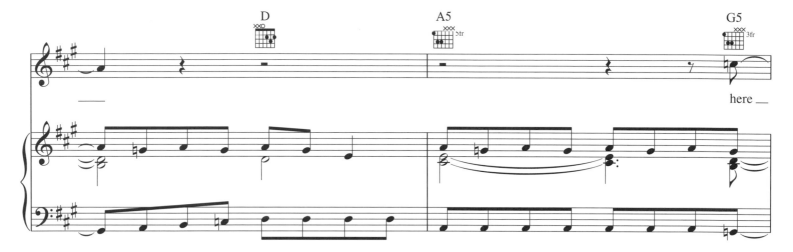

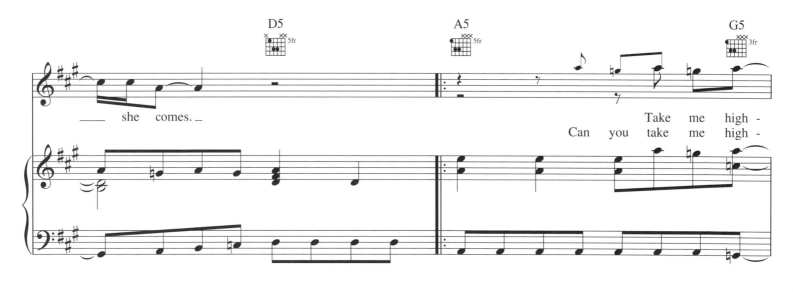

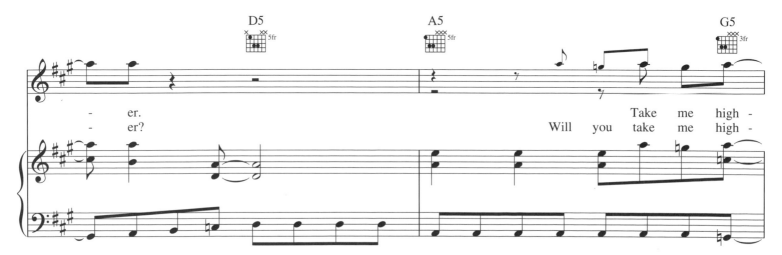

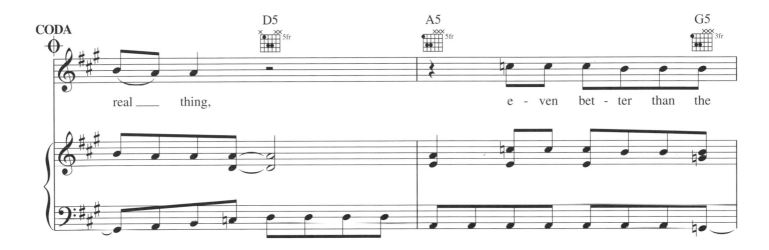

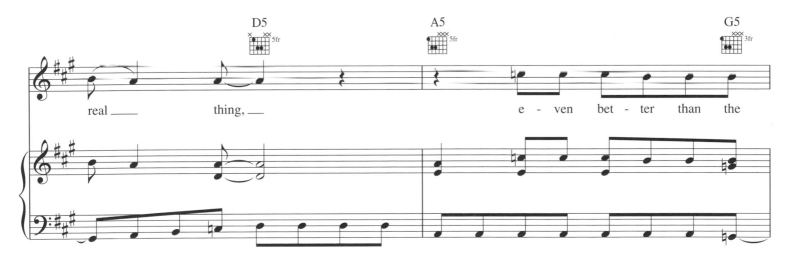

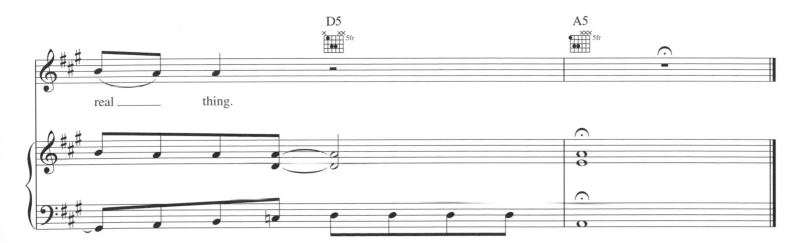

MYSTERIOUS WAYS

Lyrics by BONO and THE EDGE
Music by U2

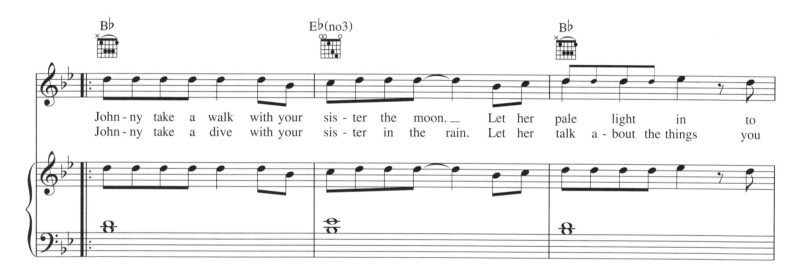

John - ny take a walk with your sis - ter the moon. __ Let her pale light in to
John - ny take a dive with your sis - ter in the rain. Let her talk a - bout the things you

fill up your room. __ You've been liv - ing un - der - ground, eat - ing from a can. __ You've been
can't ex - plain. __ To touch is to heal. To hurt is to steal. __ If you

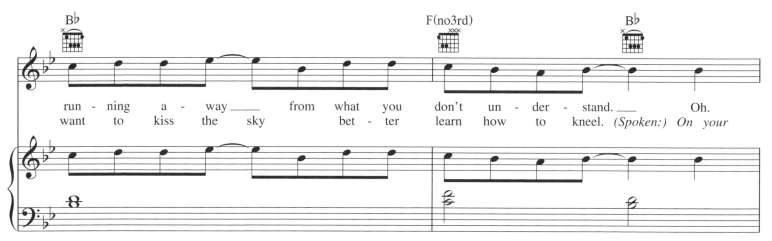

run - ning a - way ____ from what you don't un - der - stand. ____ Oh.
want to kiss the sky bet - ter learn how to kneel. *(Spoken:)* On your

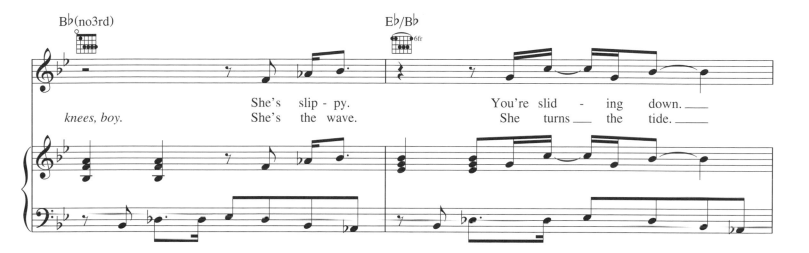

knees, boy. She's slip - py. You're slid - ing down. ____
She's the wave. She turns ____ the tide. ____

She'll be ____ there when you hit the ground. ____ }
She sees ____ a man in - side the child. ____ }

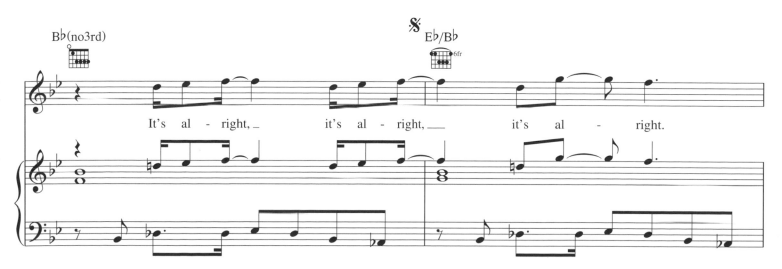

It's al - right, ____ it's al - right, ____ it's al - right.

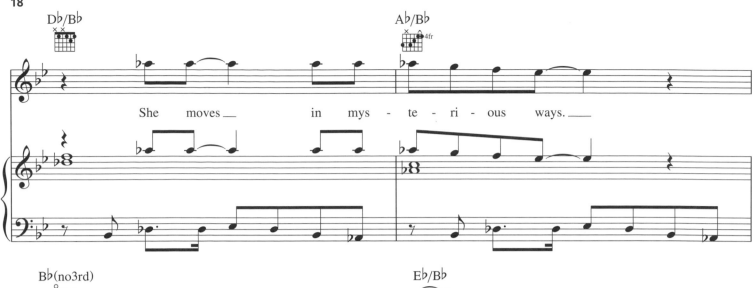

She moves __ in mys - te - ri - ous ways. __

It's al - right, __ it's al - right, __ it's al - right.

She moves __ in mys - te - ri - ous ways. __ Oh. __

te - ri - ous ways, __ yeah.

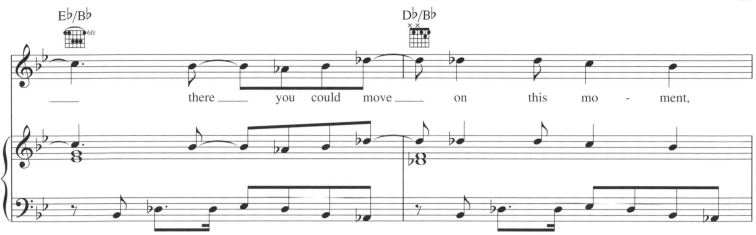

there _____ you could move _____ on this mo - ment,

fol - low this feel - ing. _____ It's al - right, _ it's al - right, _

D.S. al Coda

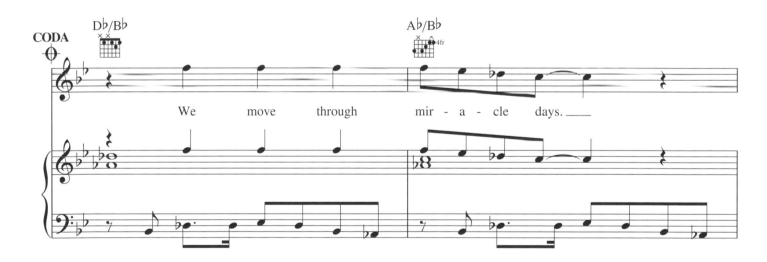

CODA

We move through mir - a - cle days. _____

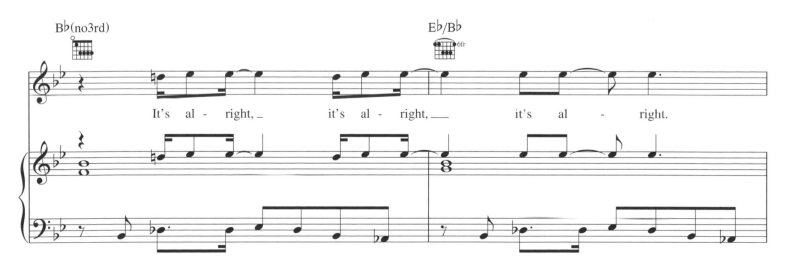

It's al - right, _ it's al - right, _____ it's al - right.

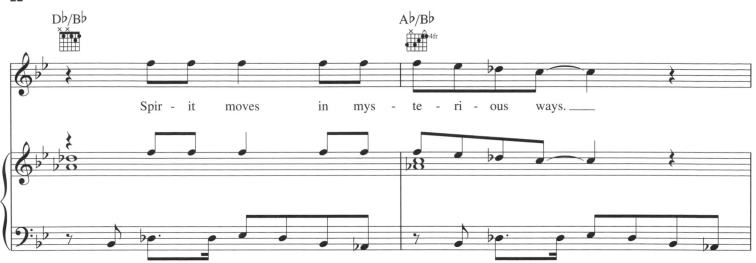

Spir - it moves in mys - te - ri - ous ways. ___

She moves ___ with it.   She moves ___ with it.

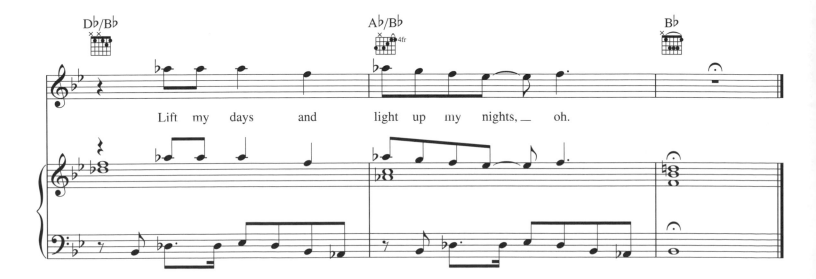

Lift my days and light up my nights, ___ oh.

BEAUTIFUL DAY

Lyrics by BONO
Music by U2

Moderately

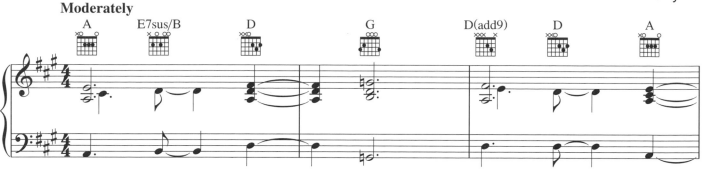

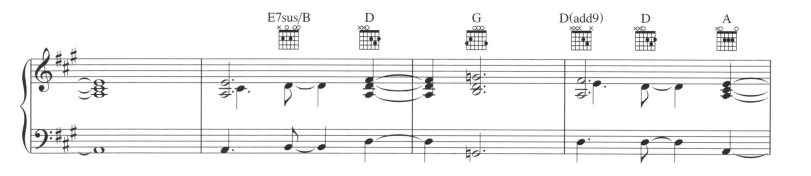

The heart is a bloom, __ shoots

up through the ston-y ground. __ But there's no room, __

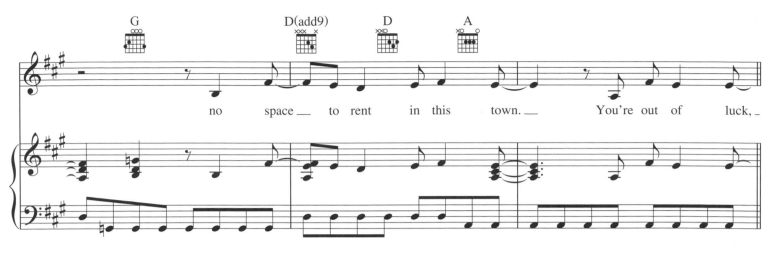

no space ___ to rent in this town. ___ You're out of luck, ___

and the rea-son that you had ___ to care, ___
but you've got ___ no ___ des - ti - na-

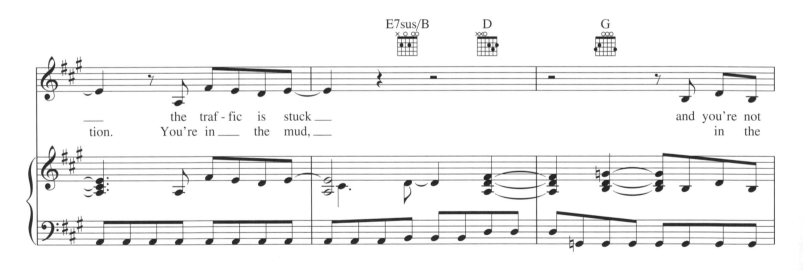

___ the traf-fic is stuck ___ and you're not
tion. You're in ___ the mud, ___ in the

mov - in' a - ny - where. You thought you'd found ___ a friend ___
maze of her i - mag - i - na - tion. You love this town ___

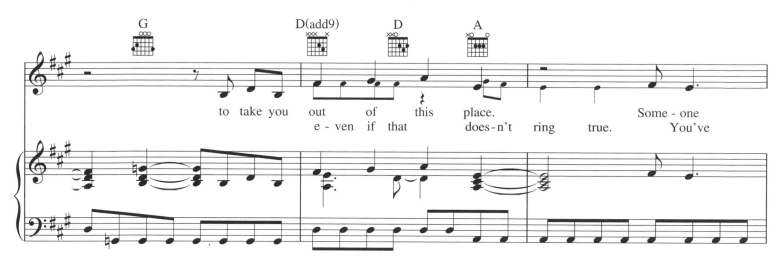

to take you out of this place.
e - ven if that does-n't ring true. Some - one You've

you could lend a hand in re - turn for grace.
been all o - ver and it's been all o - ver

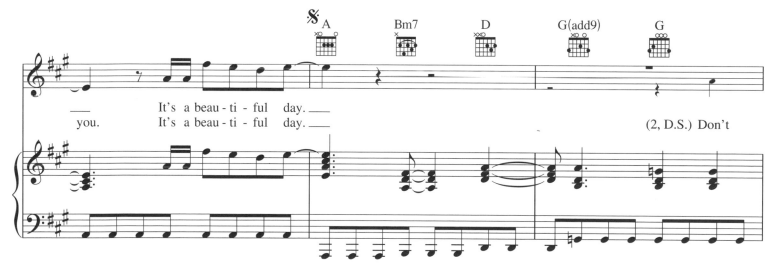

It's a beau-ti-ful day.
you. It's a beau-ti-ful day. (2, D.S.) Don't

The sky falls. And you feel like it's a beau-ti-ful day.
let it get a - way. A beau-ti-ful day.

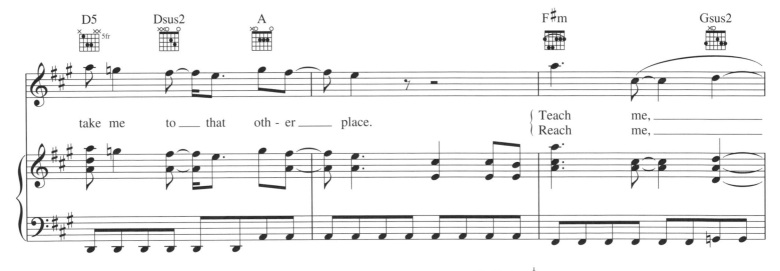

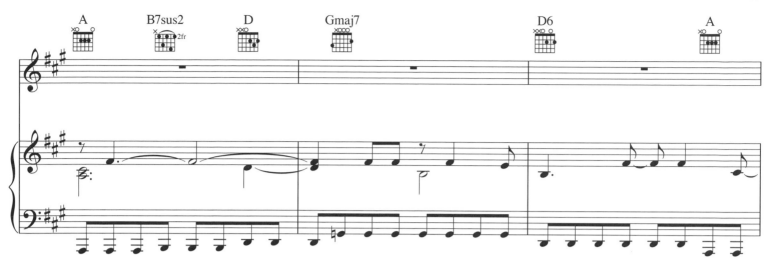

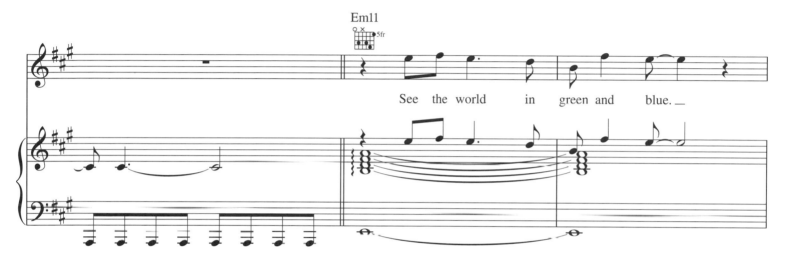

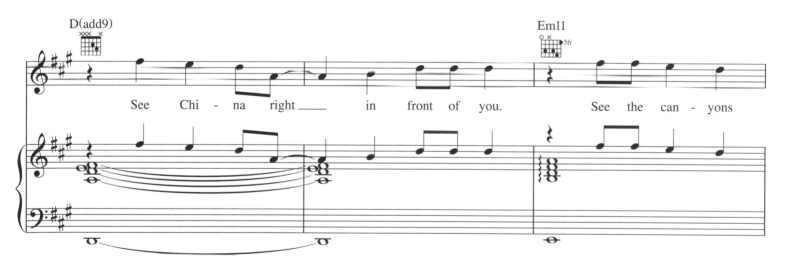

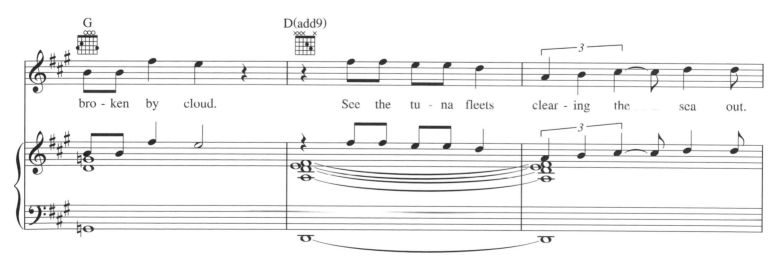

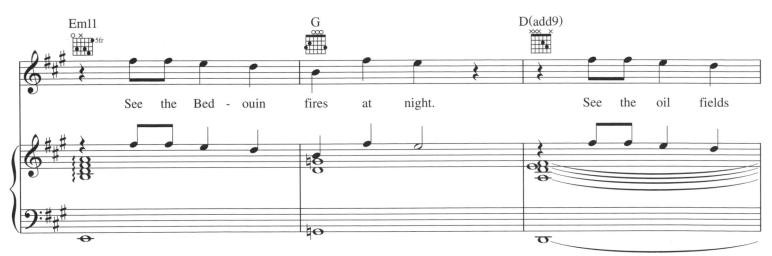

See the Bed - ouin fires at night. See the oil fields

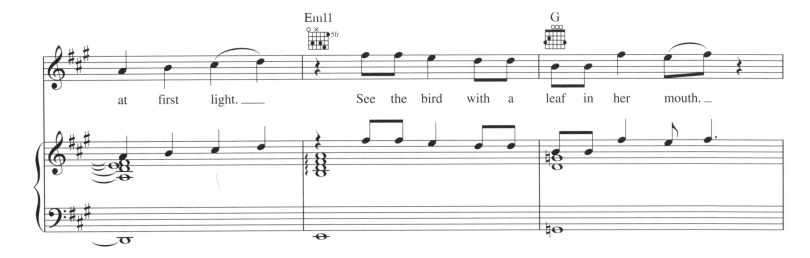

at first light. ___ See the bird with a leaf in her mouth. ___

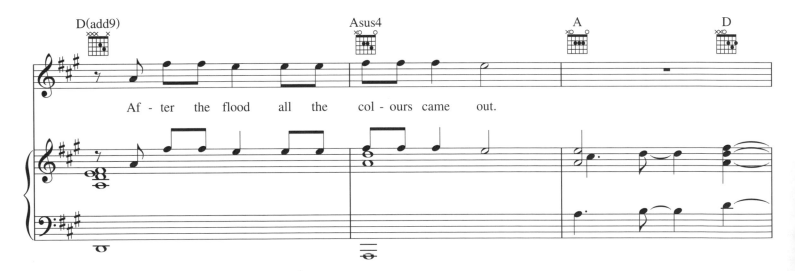

Af - ter the flood all the col - ours came out.

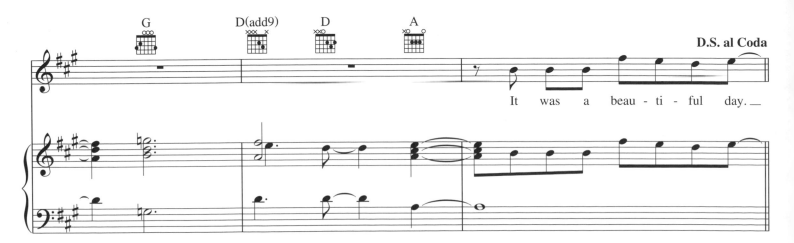

D.S. al Coda

It was a beau - ti - ful day. __

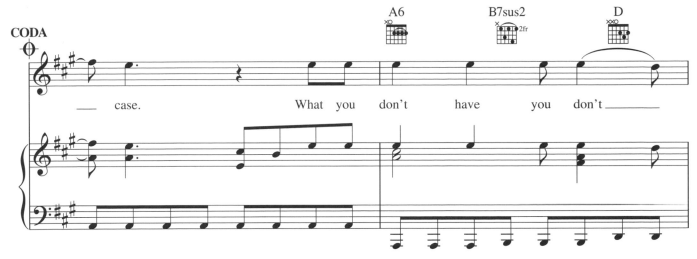

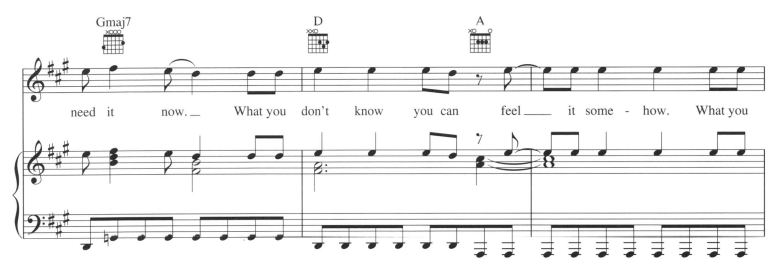

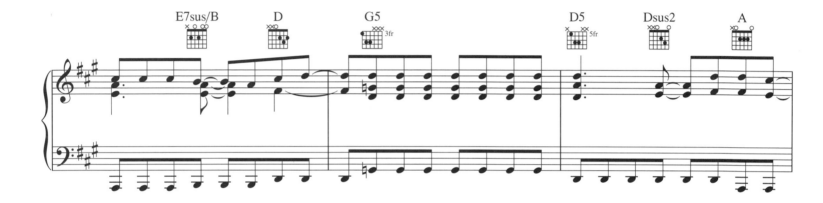

ELECTRICAL STORM

Lyrics by BONO
Music by U2

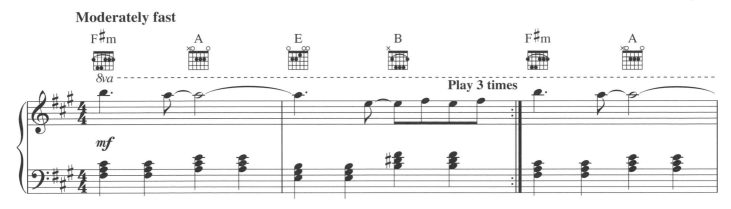

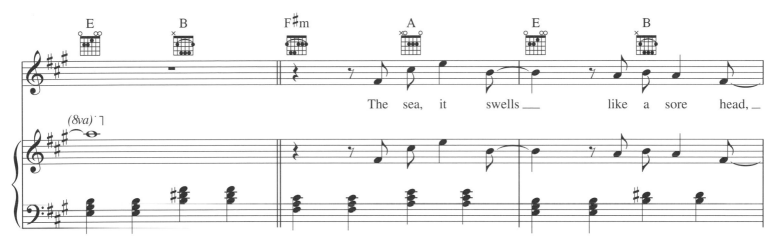

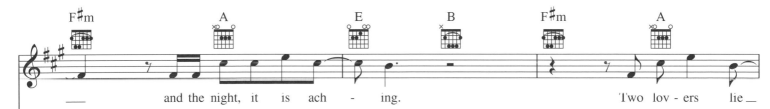

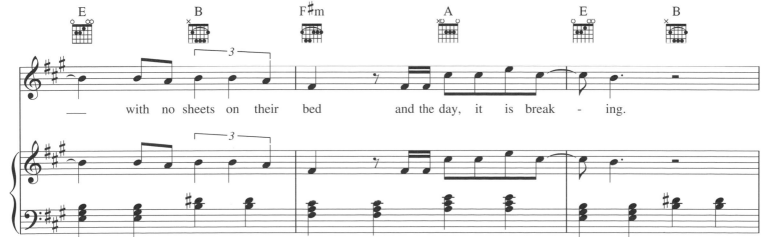

The sea, it swells like a sore head, and the night, it is ach - ing. Two lov - ers lie with no sheets on their bed and the day, it is break - ing.

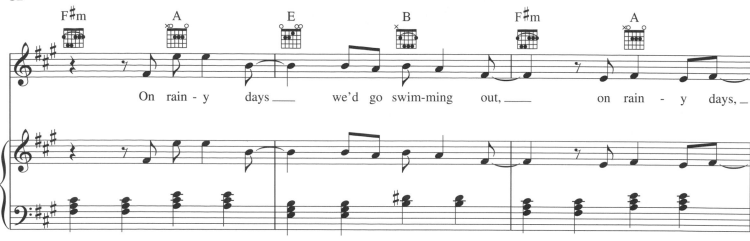

On rain-y days ___ we'd go swim-ming out, ___ on rain-y days, ___

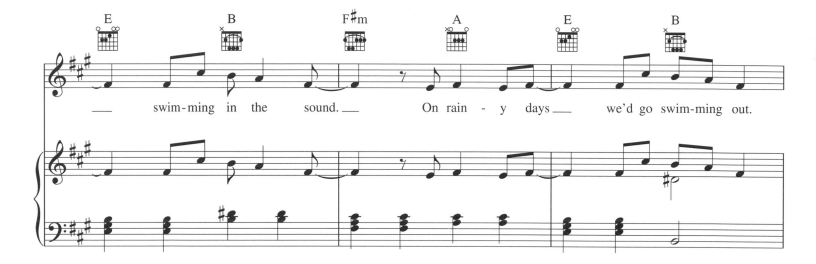

___ swim-ming in the sound. ___ On rain - y days ___ we'd go swim-ming out.

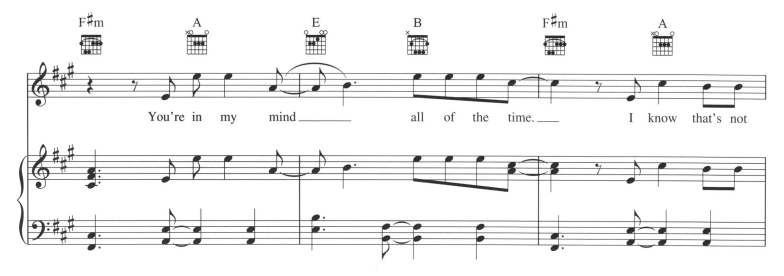

You're in my mind ___ all of the time. ___ I know that's not

e - nough. ___ If the sky can crack, there must be some way back ___

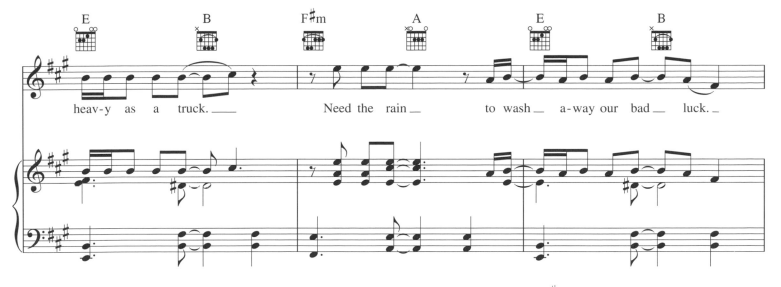

heav-y as a truck. _____ Need the rain _____ to wash _____ a-way our bad _____ luck. _____

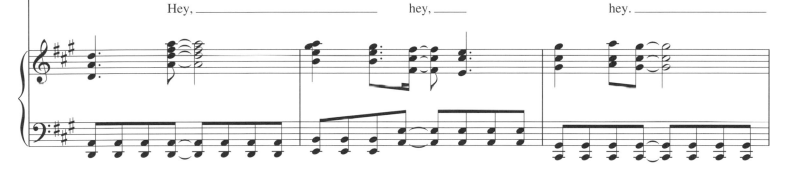

Hey, _____ hey, _____ hey. _____

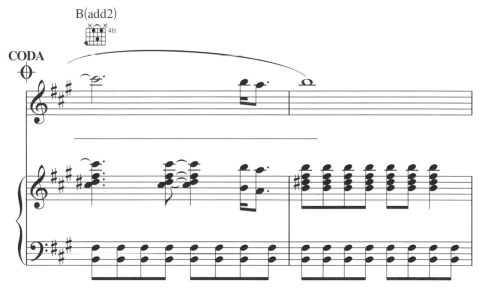

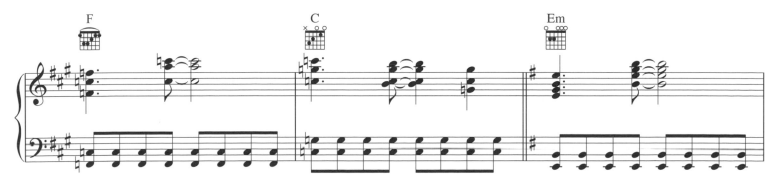

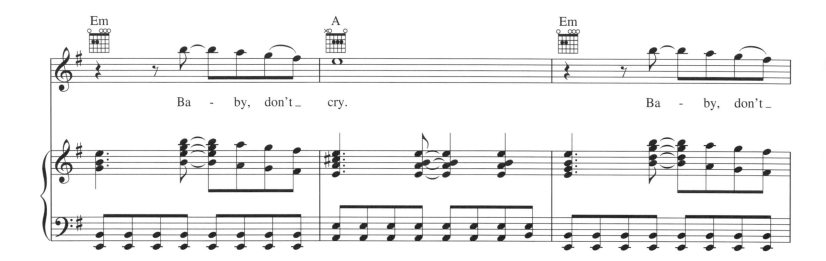

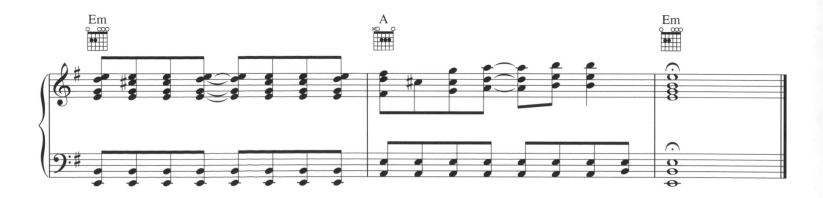

ONE

Lyrics by BONO and THE EDGE
Music by U2

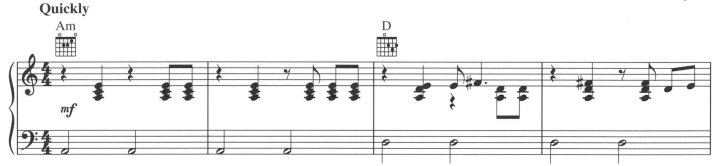

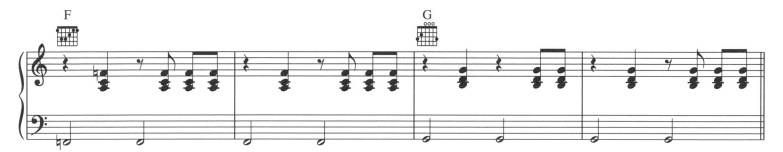

Is it get-ting bet-ter
Did I dis-ap - point you
Have you come here for for - give-ness?

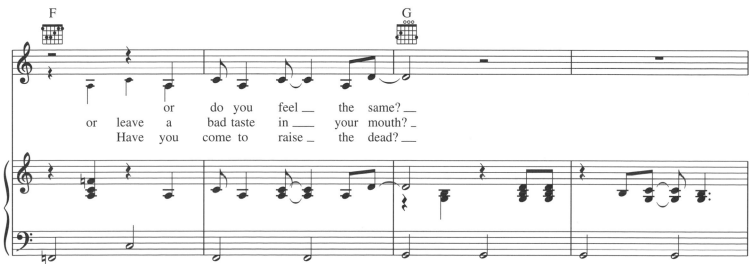

or do you feel __ the same? __
or leave a bad taste in __ your mouth? __
Have you come to raise __ the dead? __

Will it make it eas - i - er on ___ you now?
You act like you nev - er had love
Have you come here to play Je - sus

You got ___ some - one ___ to blame. ___ You said
and you want me to go ___ with - out. ___ Well, it's
to the lep - ers in ___ your head? ___ Did I

one love, ___ one life, ___
too late ___ to - night ___
ask too much, ___ more than a lot?

when it's one need ___ in the night. ___
to drag the past ___ out in - to the light. ___
You gave me ___ noth - in', now it's all I got.

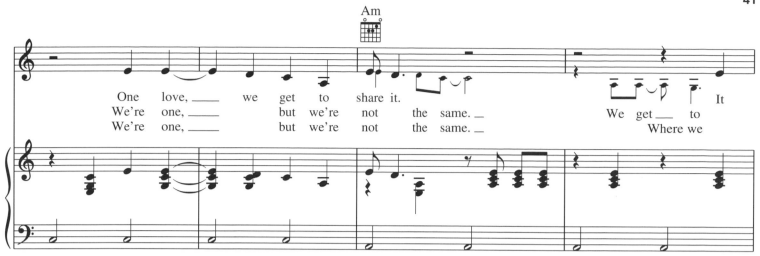

One love, ___ we get to share it.
We're one, ___ but we're not the same. __
We're one, ___ but we're not the same. __
We get ___ to
Where we
It

leaves you, ba - by, if you don't care for it. ___
car - ry each oth - er, car - ry each oth - er.
hurt each oth - er, and we're do - in' it a - gain.

One. ___

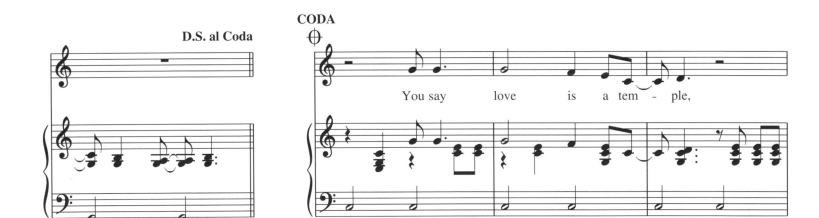

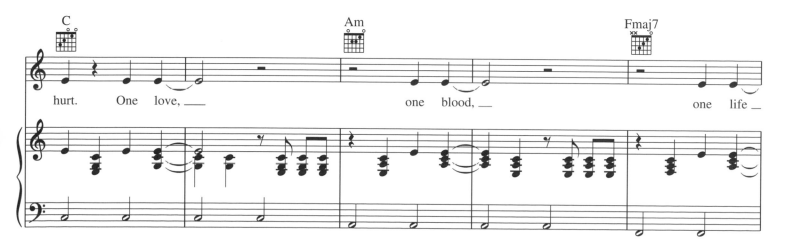

you've got to do what you should. ___ One life ___

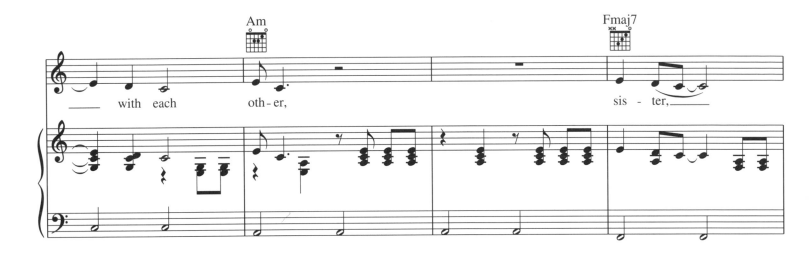

___ with each oth-er, sis - ter, ___

broth-ers. One life, ___

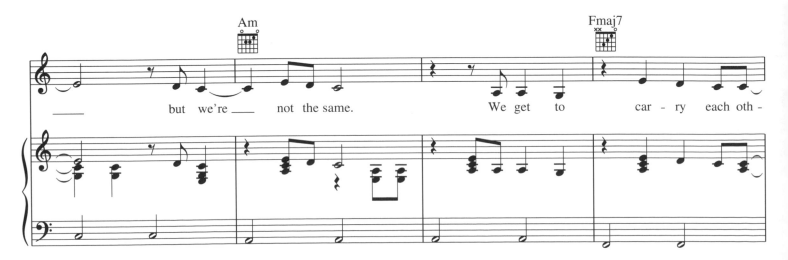

___ but we're ___ not the same. We get to car - ry each oth-

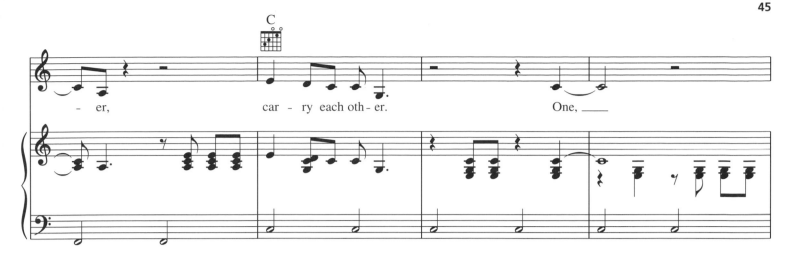

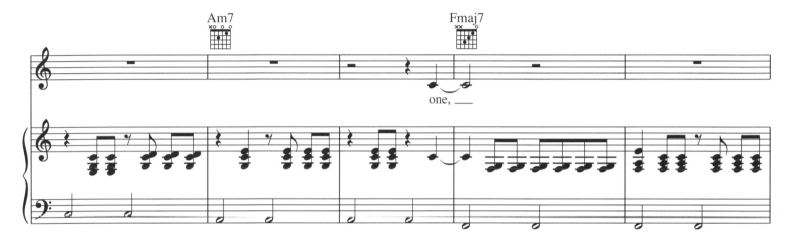

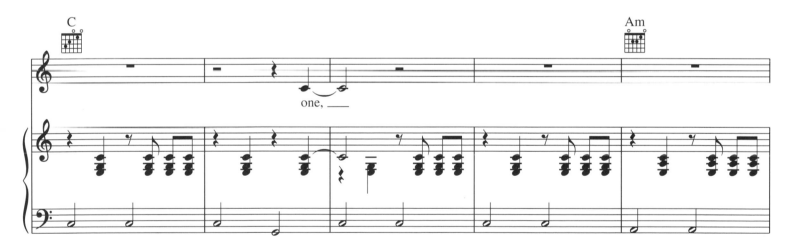

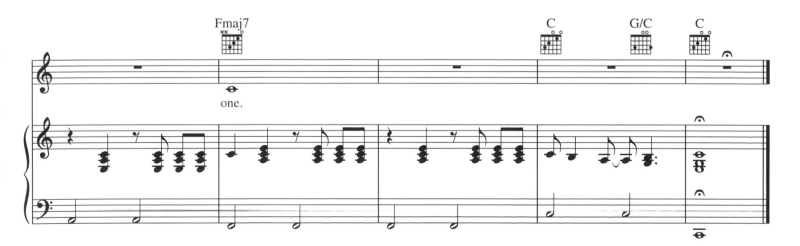

MISS SARAJEVO

Lyrics by BONO and THE EDGE
Music by U2

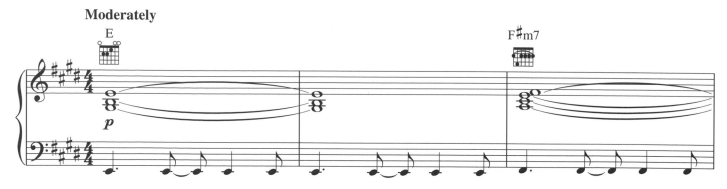

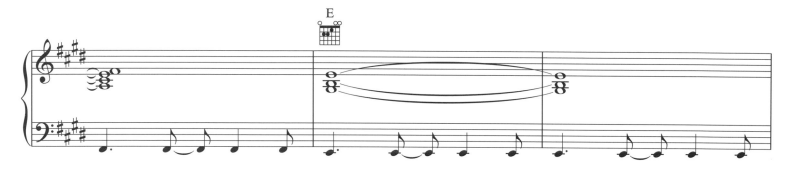

Is there a time ___ for keep-ing a dis-
___ to run for cov-

- tance, a time ___ to turn your eyes a - way? ___ Is there a time ___
- er, a time ___ for kiss and tell? ___ Is there a time ___

48

vi - a al ma - re. _____ E come il fiu - me _____

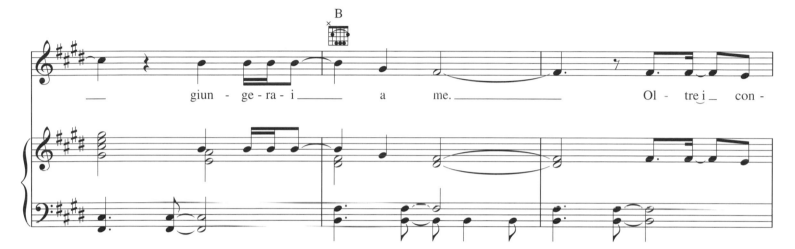

_____ giun - ge - ra - i _____ a me. _____ Ol - tre i con -

fi - ni, _____ e le ter - re as - se - ta - te. _____

_____ Di - ci che co - me fiu - me _____ co -

-me fiu - me _____ l'a - mo -

- re giun - ger - a, _____ l'a -

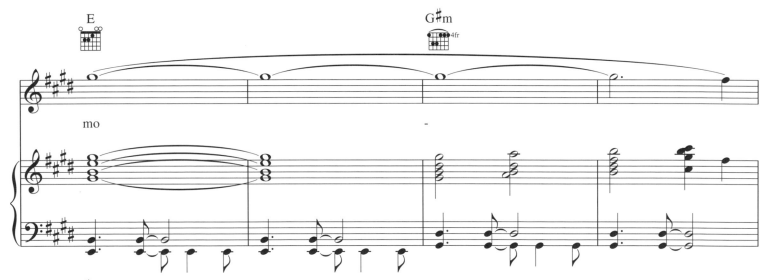

mo - _____

re.   E non __ so pi ___ pre - gare.

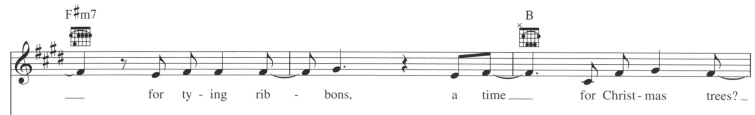

Is there a time ___ for lay-ing ___ ta - bles when the night ___

is set to freeze? ___

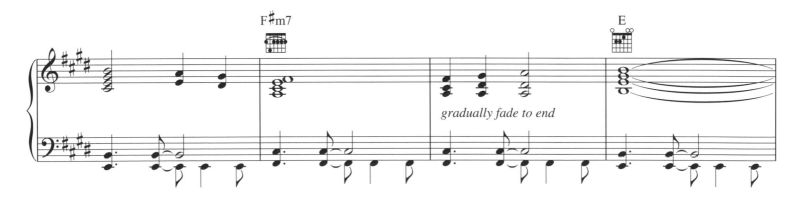

gradually fade to end

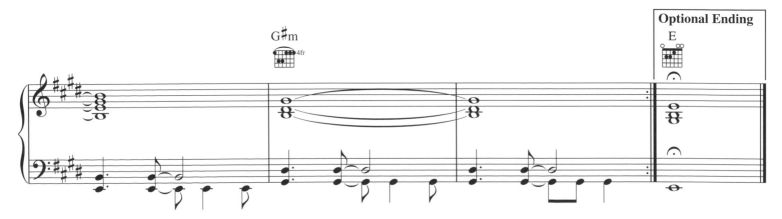

Optional Ending

STAY
(Faraway, So Close!)

Lyrics by BONO and THE EDGE
Music by U2

Dressed up ____ like a car ____ crash, the
round. You used to stay in to watch the ad - verts. You

wheels are turn - ing but you're up - side down. ____ You say when ____ he
could lip - sync ____ to ____ the

hits you, you don't mind, _____

be - cause when ____ he hurts you, ____ you feel a - live. _____ Hey ____

57

STUCK IN A MOMENT YOU CAN'T GET OUT OF

Lyrics by BONO and THE EDGE
Music by U2

Moderately slow

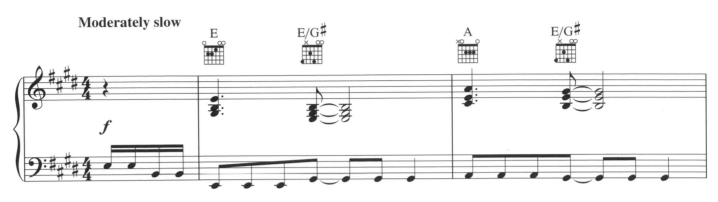

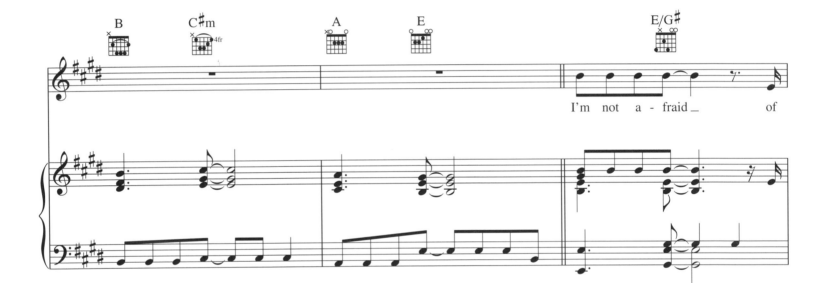

have-n't al - read-y heard. ___ I'm just try-in' to find ___ a de -

- cent mel - o - dy, ___ a song ___ that I can sing ___ in my

own com - pa - ny. You've got to get your-self to - geth - er. You got

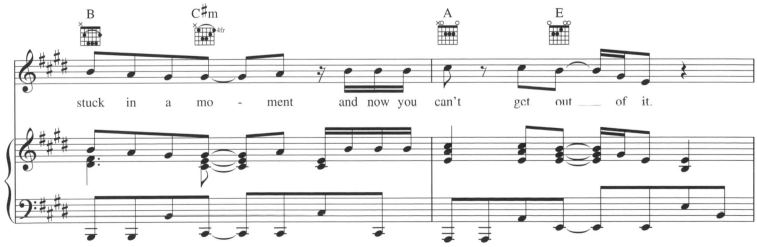

stuck in a mo - ment and now you can't get out ___ of it.

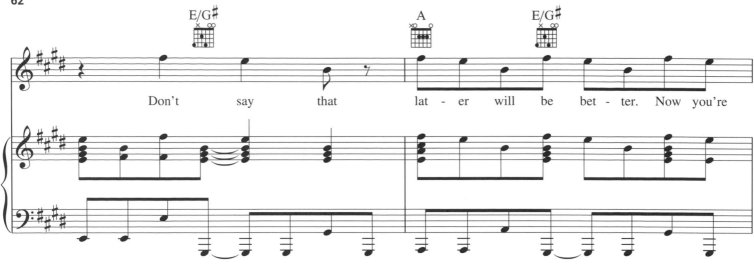

Don't say that lat-er will be bet-ter. Now you're

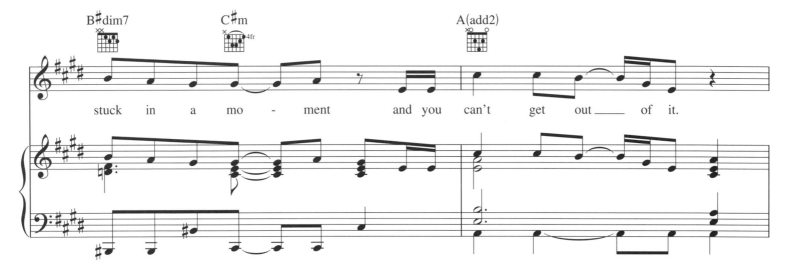

stuck in a mo-ment and you can't get out ___ of it.

I will not ___ for-sake ___ the col -

- ors that you bring, ___ the nights ___ you filled with fire-works they, they

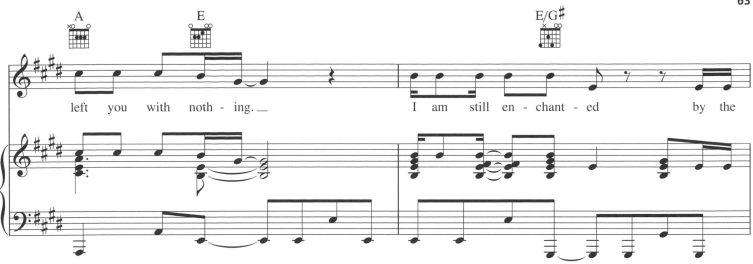

left you with noth-ing.___ I am still en-chant-ed by the

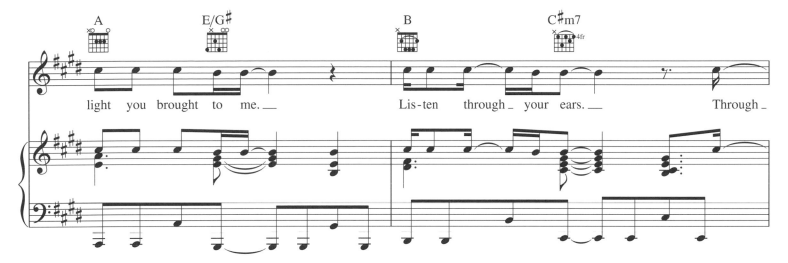

light you brought to me.___ Lis-ten through___ your ears.___ Through___

___ your eyes I could see. You are such a fool

to wor-ry like___ you do. Oh._____ I know it's tough,___

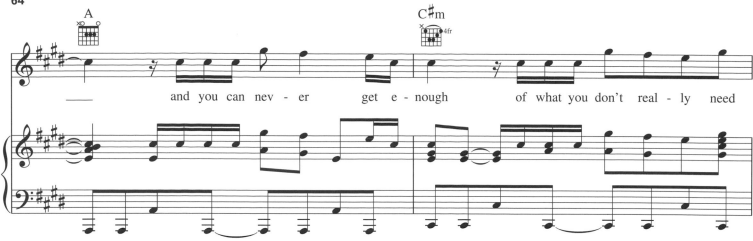

and you can nev - er get e - nough of what you don't real - ly need

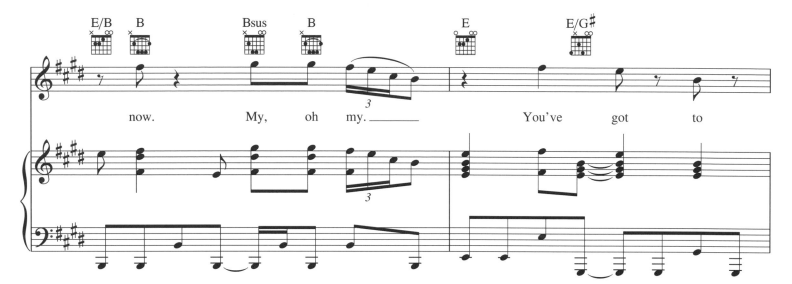

now. My, oh my. _____ You've got to

get your - self to - geth - er. You've got stuck in a mo - ment and you

can't get out ___ of it. Oh Lord,

look at you now;___ you've got your-self stuck in a mo - ment and you

can't get out___ of it. I was un-con - scious, half___ a-sleep. The

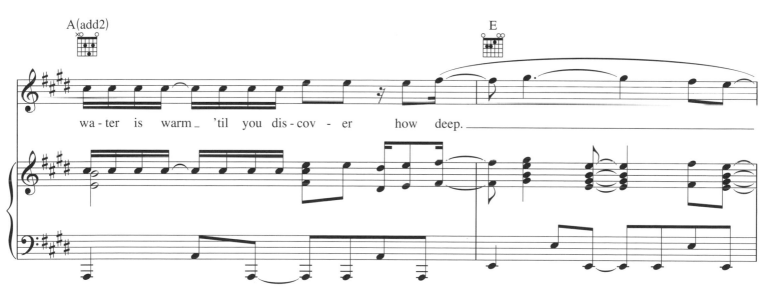

wa - ter is warm___ 'til you dis-cov - er how deep._____

I was-n't jump - ing; for me it was a fall. It's a

long way down to noth - ing at all. _____ Oh hey,

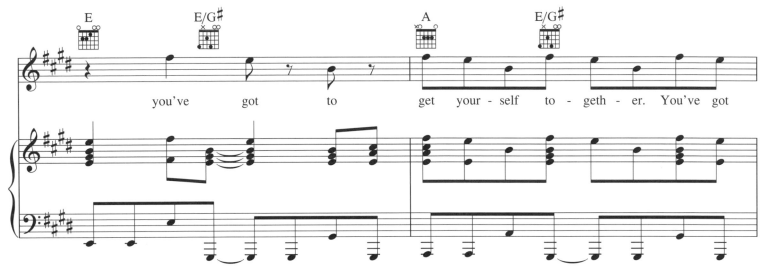

you've got to get your - self to - geth - er. You've got

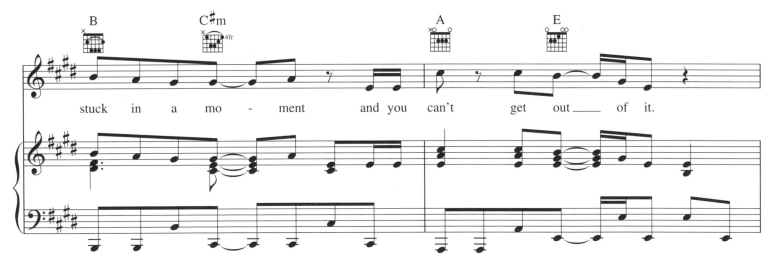

stuck in a mo - ment and you can't get out ___ of it.

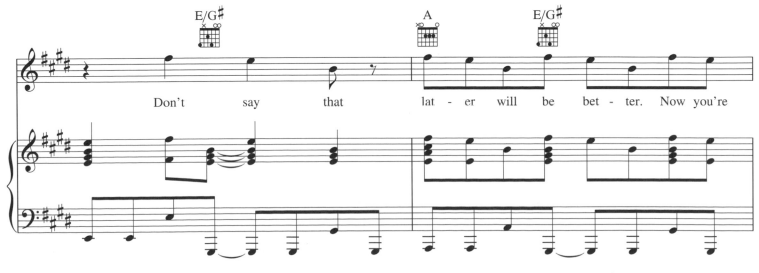

Don't say that lat - er will be bet - ter. Now you're

67

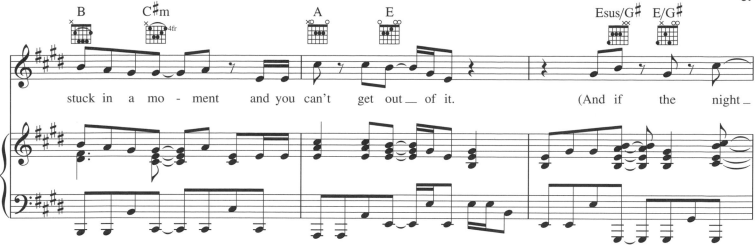

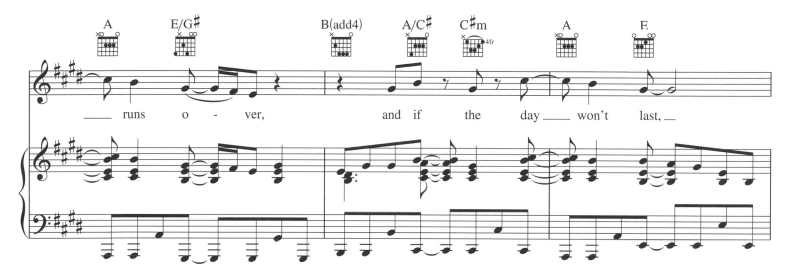

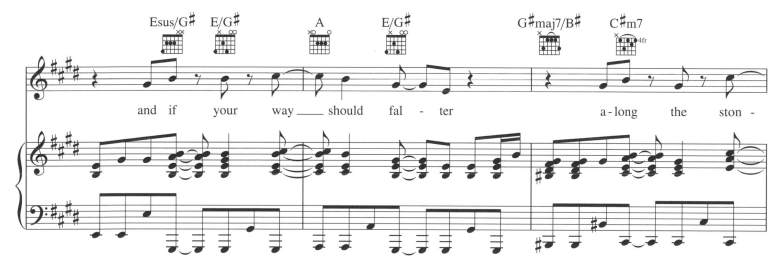

GONE

Lyrics by BONO and THE EDGE
Music by U2

Moderately

You get ___

* Recorded a step lower.

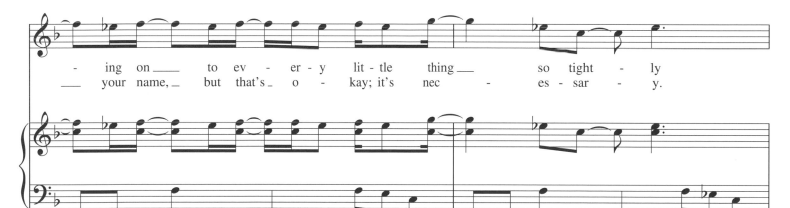

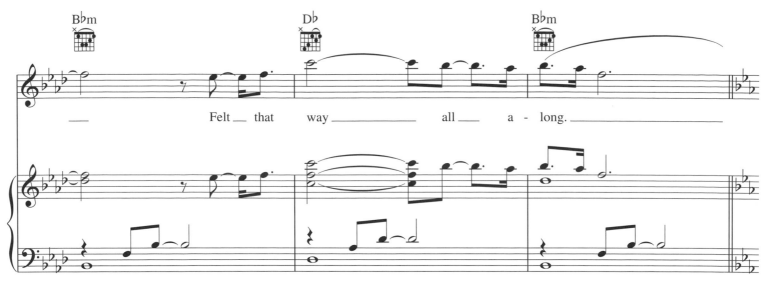

Felt __ that way _____ all __ a - long. _____

Clos-er to you ev -'ry day. __ Did -n't want it that much

an - y - way. __ You're

tak - ing steps ___ that make you __ feel diz - zy,

UNTIL THE END OF THE WORLD

Lyrics by BONO and THE EDGE
Music by U2

Moderately

Have-n't seen you in quite a while. I was

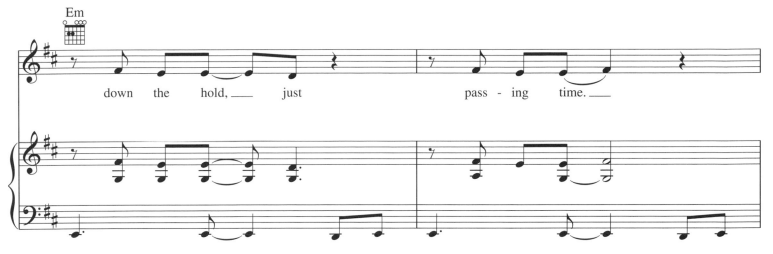

down the hold, ___ just   pass - ing time. ___

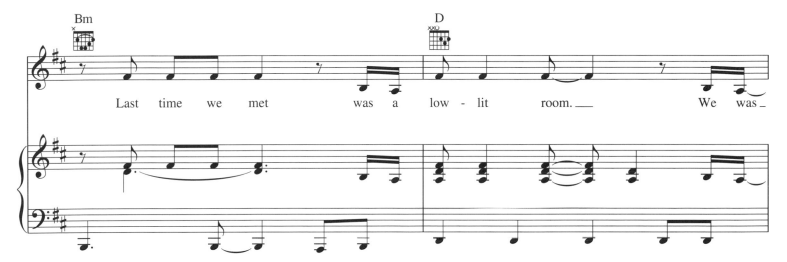

Last time we met   was a low - lit room. ___   We was ___

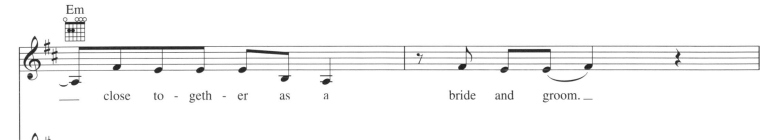

___ close to - geth - er   as a   bride and groom. ___

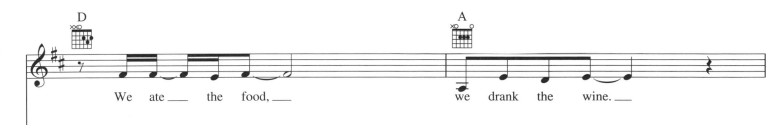

We ate ___ the food, ___   we drank the wine. ___

Ev-'ry-bod-y hav-ing a good time ex-cept you; ___

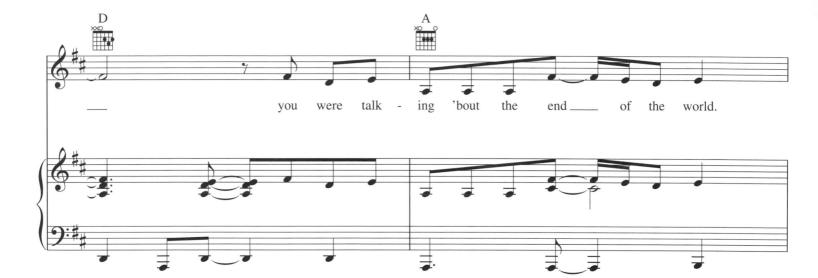

___ you were talk-ing 'bout the end ___ of the world.

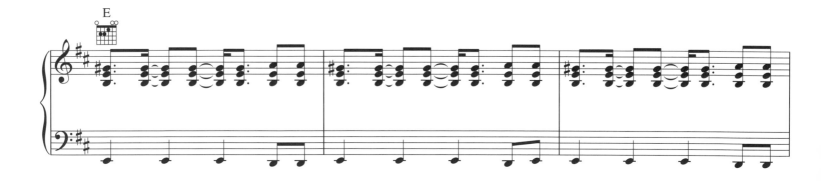

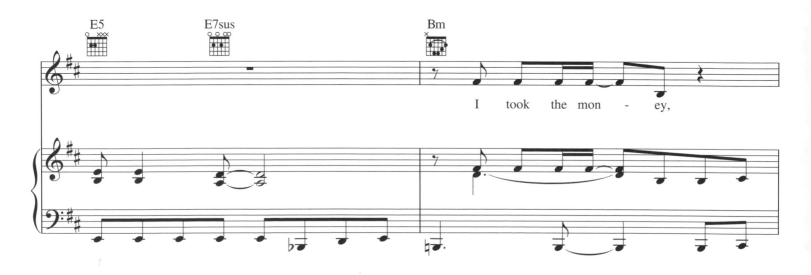

I took the mon — ey,

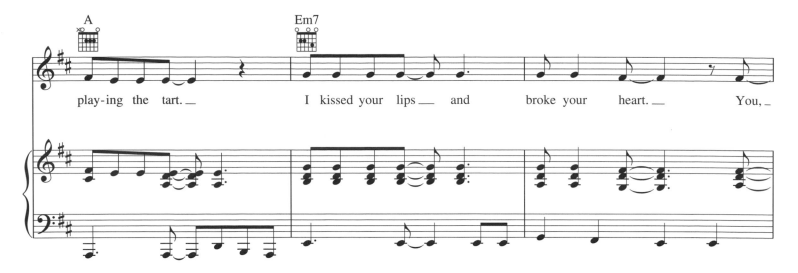

play-ing the tart. __ I kissed your lips __ and broke your heart. __ You, __

__ you were act - ing like it was the end of the world. _____

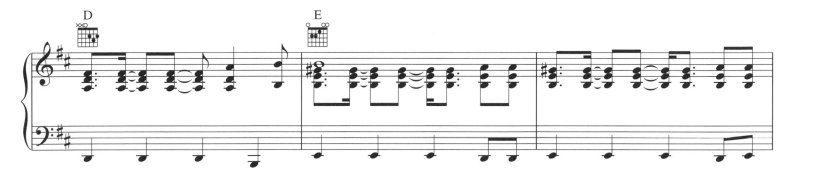

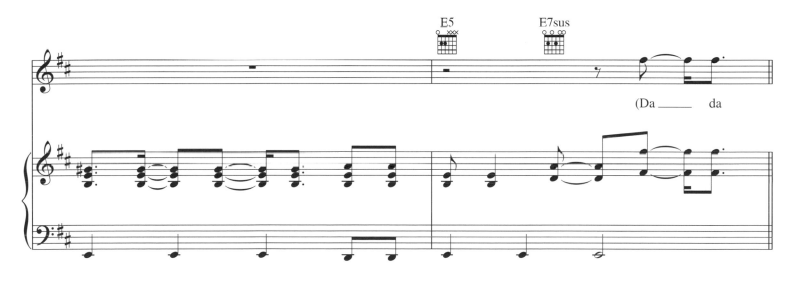

(Da _____ da

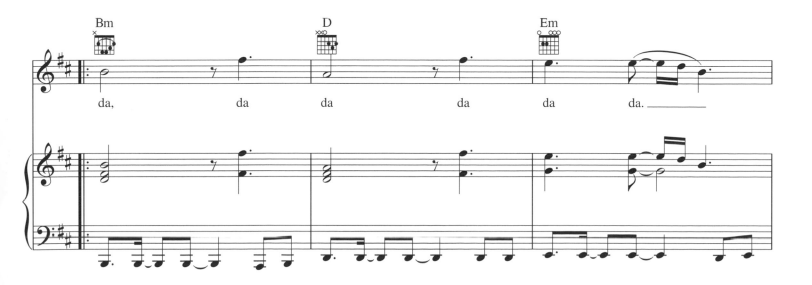

da, da da da da da. _____

Da ___ da da.) In my dream ___ I was

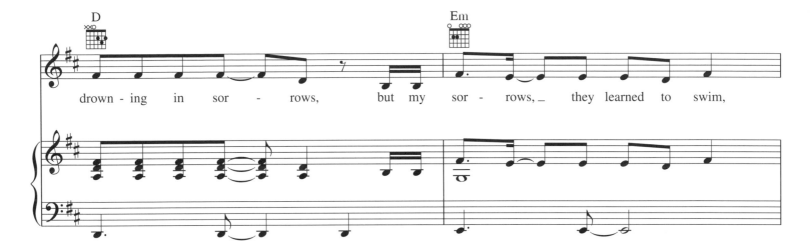

drown - ing in sor - rows, but my sor - rows, ___ they learned to swim,

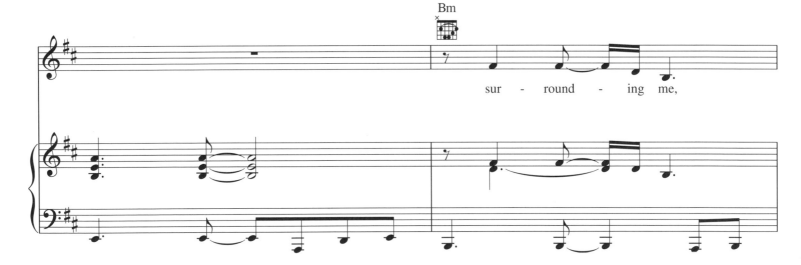

sur - round - ing me,

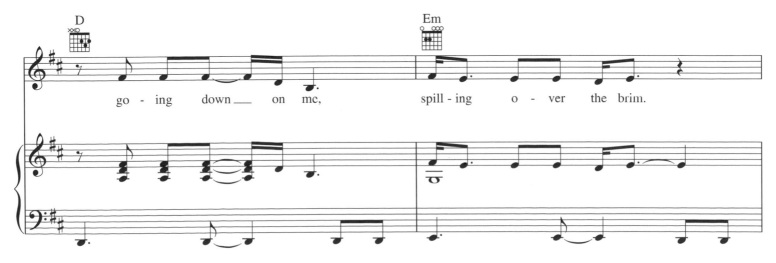

go - ing down ___ on me, spill - ing o - ver the brim.

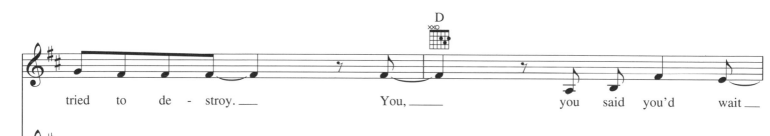

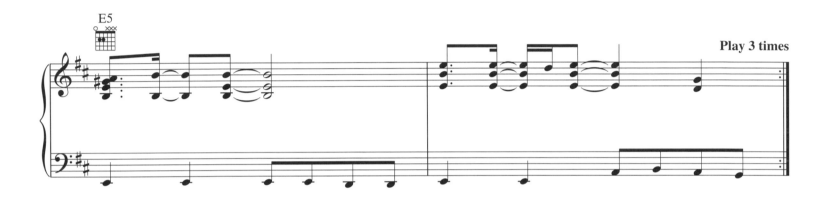

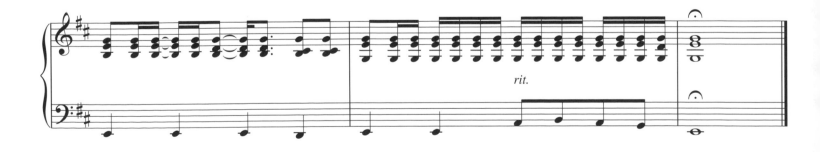

THE HANDS THAT BUILT AMERICA

Lyrics by BONO
Music by U2

from the storm - y fields ___ to hang-ing steel ___ from sky, ___
I ___ took your kiss ___ on the spray of the new line star. ___

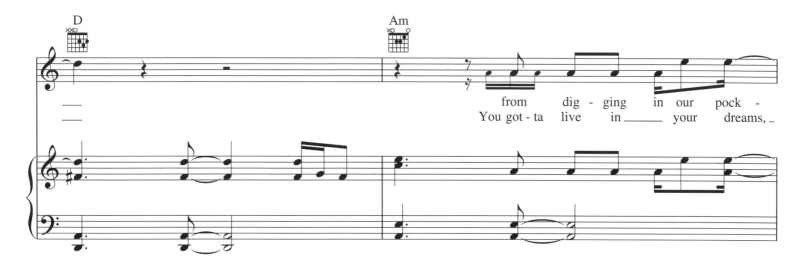

— from dig - ging in our pock -
— You got - ta live in ___ your dreams, ___

- ets for ___ a rea - son, not to say good - bye. }
___ don't make them ___ so hard, uh, ___ huh. ___ }

These are ___ the hands ___ that built A -

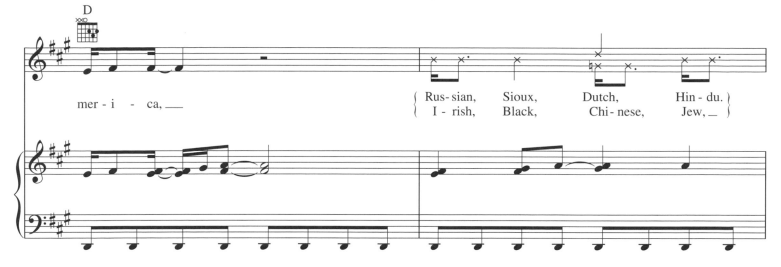

mer - i - ca, ___

Rus-sian, Sioux, Dutch, Hin-du.
I-rish, Black, Chi-nese, Jew, ___

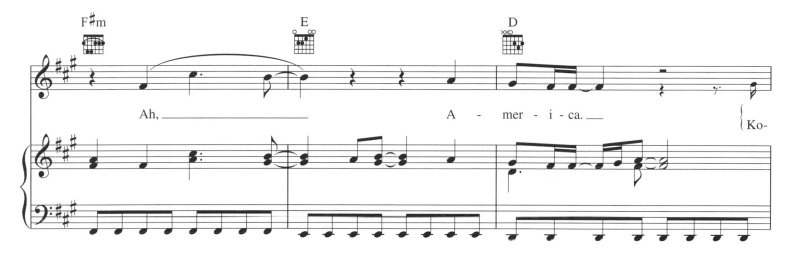

Ah, _____ A - mer - i - ca. ___ {Ko-

Pol-ish, I-rish, Ger-man, I-tal-ian.
re-an, His-pan-ic, Mus-lim, In-di-an.

Of all _____ of the

prom - is - es, ___ is this one _____ we could

keep? _____ Of all of the

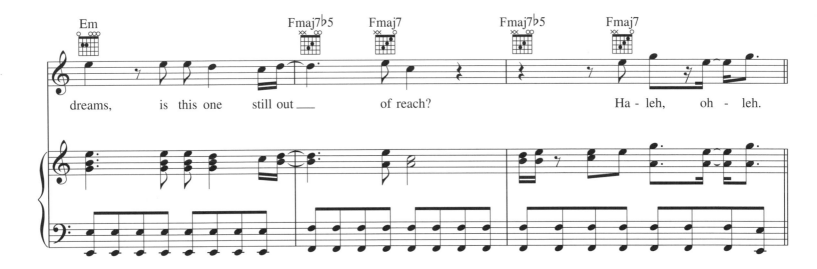

dreams, is this one still out ___ of reach? Ha - leh, oh - leh.

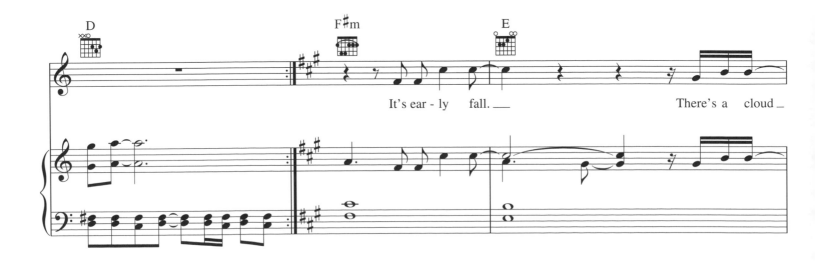

It's ear - ly fall. ___ There's a cloud ___

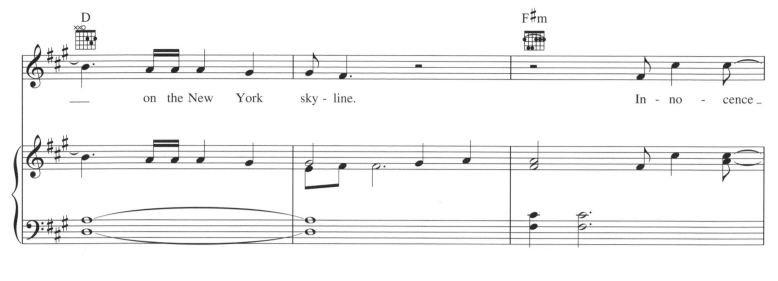

on the New York sky-line. In-no-cence

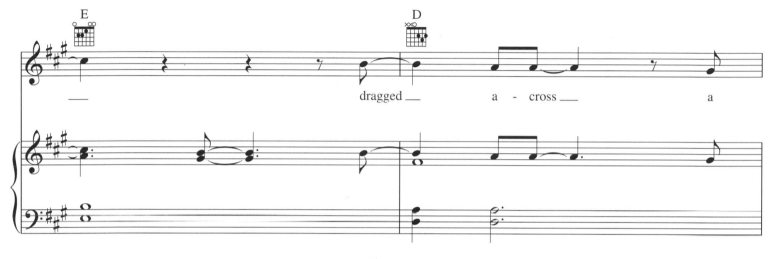

dragged a-cross a

yel-low line. These are the hands

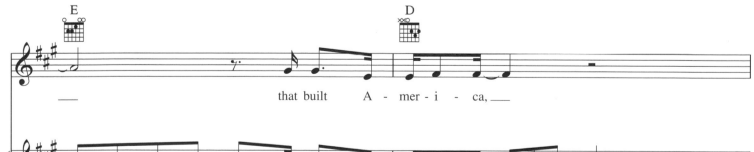

that built A-mer-i-ca,

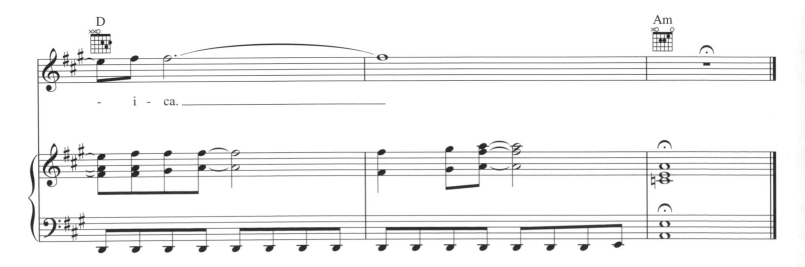

DISCOTHÈQUE

Lyrics by BONO and THE EDGE
Music by U2

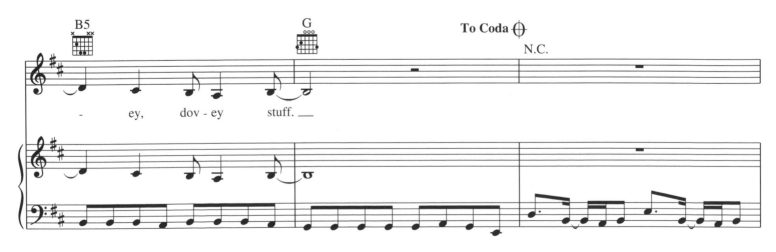

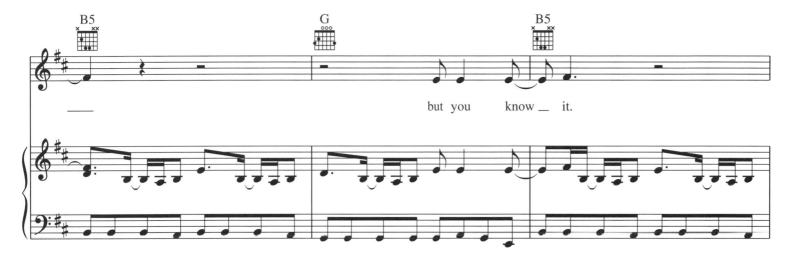

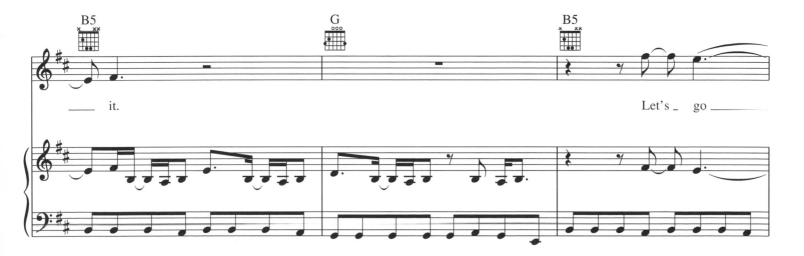

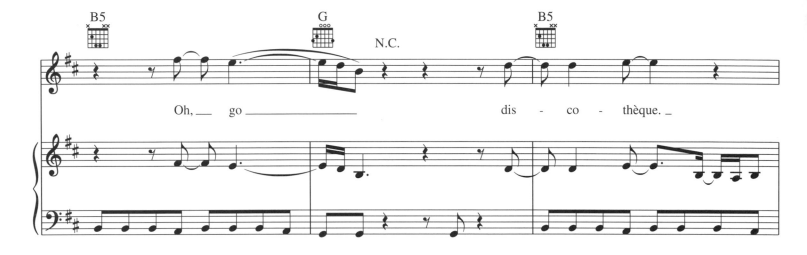

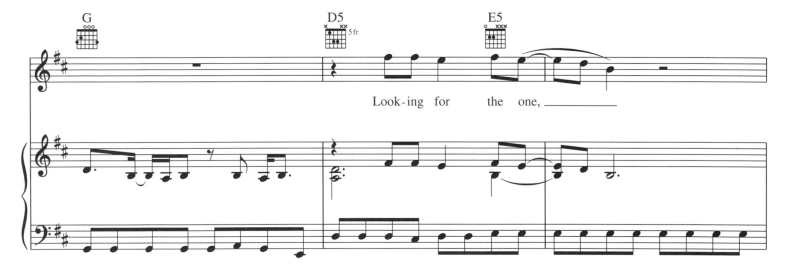

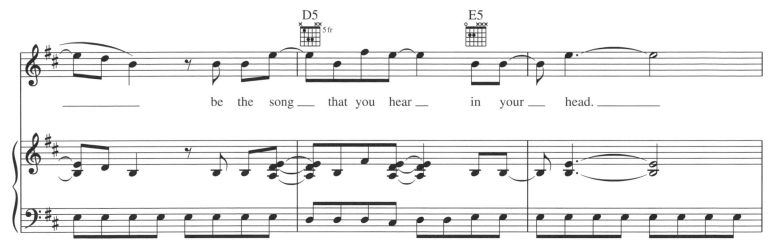

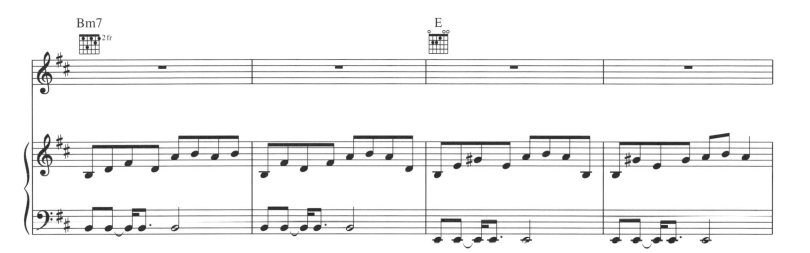

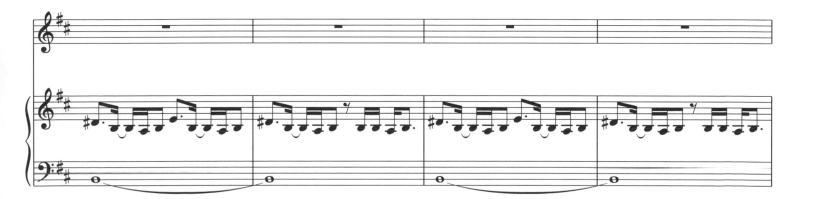

D.S. al Coda
(take 2nd ending)

It's no ____ trick, _

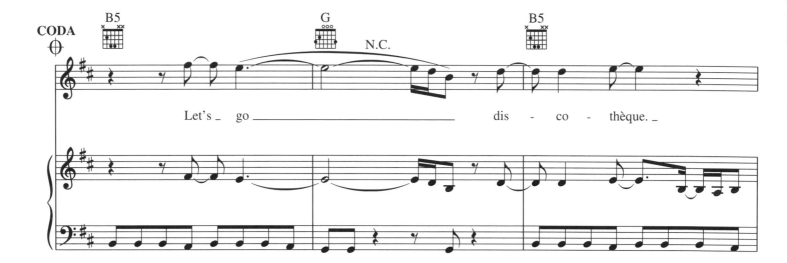

Let's _ go _____ dis - co - thèque. _

Go, ___ go,   ah, _____ dis -
Vocal 1st time only

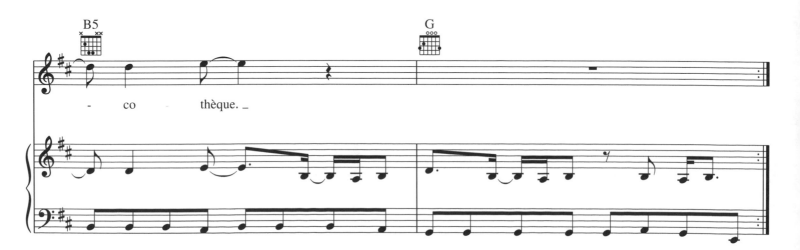

- co   thèque. _

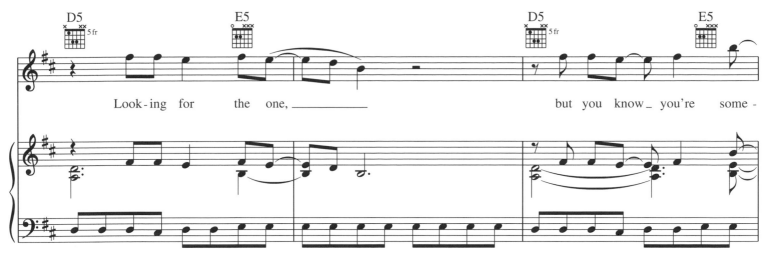

Look-ing for the one, _____ but you know_ you're some-

- where else_ in - stead. Wan - na be the song, _____ be the song,_

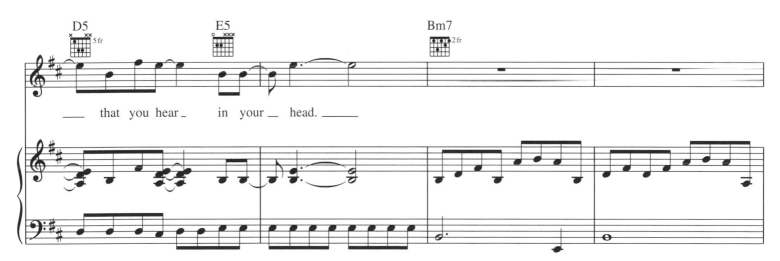

___ that you hear_ in your _ head. _____

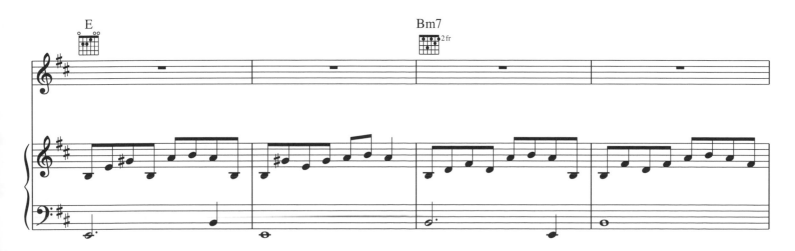

But you take ___ what you ___ can get ___

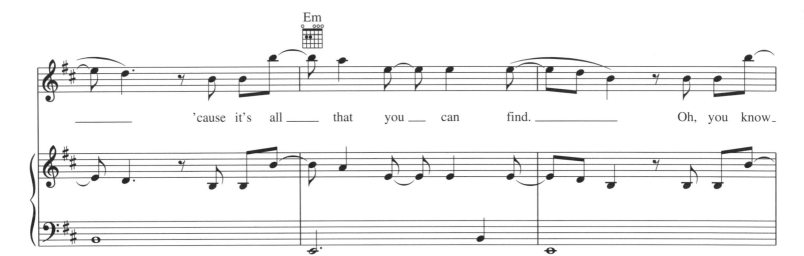

___ 'cause it's all ___ that you ___ can find. ___ Oh, you know ___

___ there's some - thing more ___ but to - night, ___ to - night, ___ to - night.

Repeat and Fade

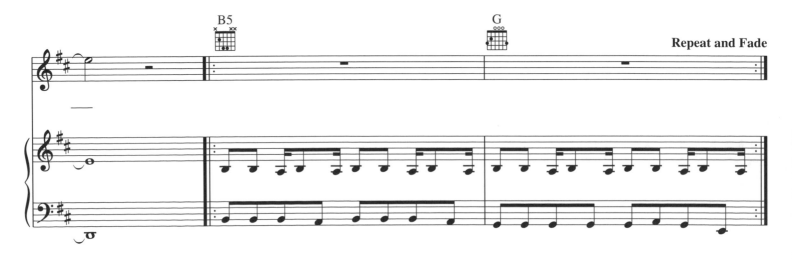

HOLD ME, THRILL ME, KISS ME, KILL ME

Lyrics by BONO and THE EDGE
Music by U2

don't know how you took it, you just know what you got. _ Oh,

lawd - y, you been steal - ing from the thieves and you got caught._ In the

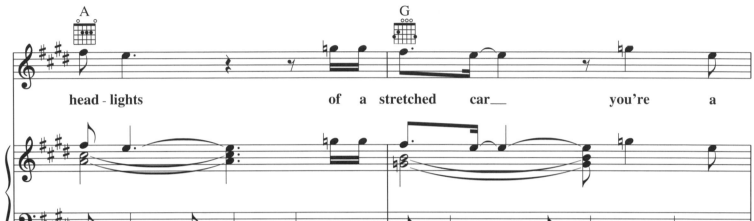

head - lights of a stretched car___ you're a

star.

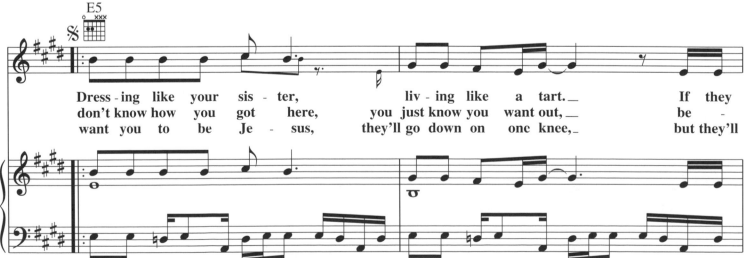

Dress - ing like your sis - ter, liv - ing like a tart._ If they
don't know how you got here, you just know you want out, __ be -
want you to be Je - sus, they'll go down on one knee,_ but they'll

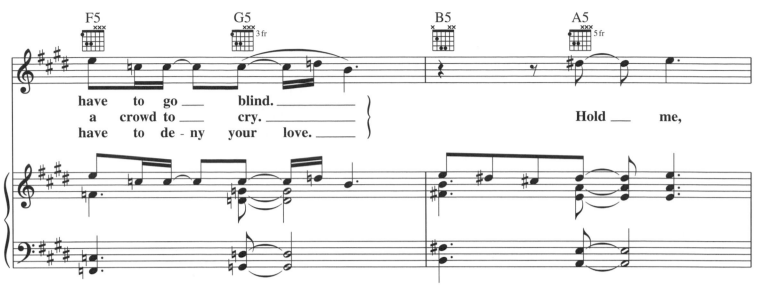

have to go ___ blind. _____
a crowd to ___ cry. _____
have to de-ny your love. _____

Hold ___ me,

To Coda ⊕

thrill ___ me,   kiss ___ me,

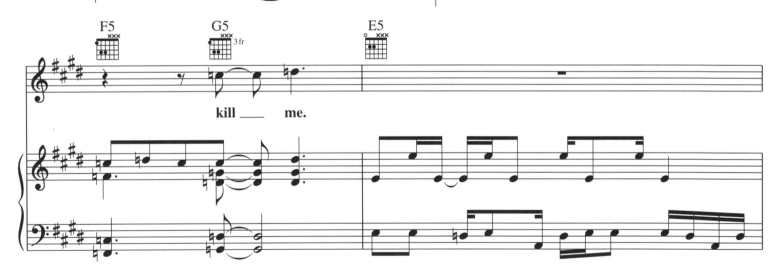

kill ___ me.

You

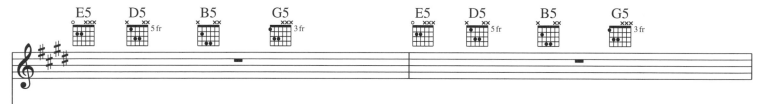

D.S. al Coda

They

104

kill ___ me. ____

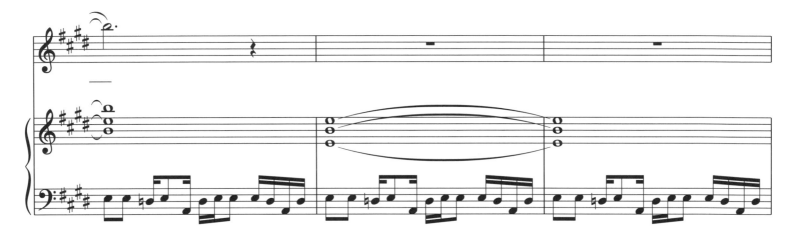

Repeat and Fade

STARING AT THE SUN

Lyrics by BONO and THE EDGE
Music by U2

Slow Rock Ballad

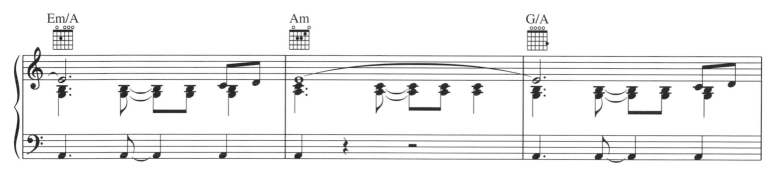

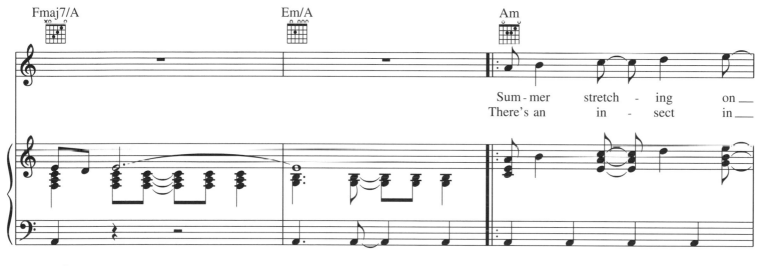

Sum-mer stretch-ing on ___
There's an in - sect in ___

___ the grass.... ___ sum - mer dress - es pass, ___ pass, _____
___ your ear. ___ If you scratch, it won't dis - ap - pear. It's

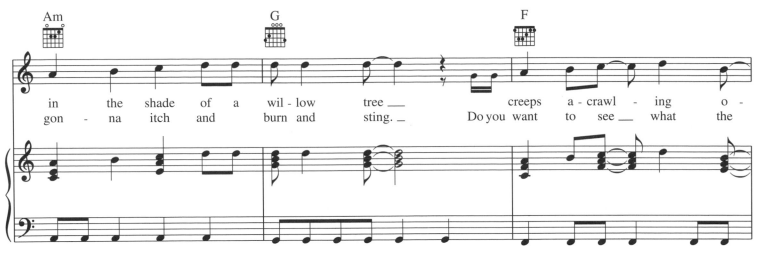

in the shade of a wil - low tree ___ creeps a-crawl - ing o -
gon - na itch and burn and sting. ___ Do you want to see ___ what the

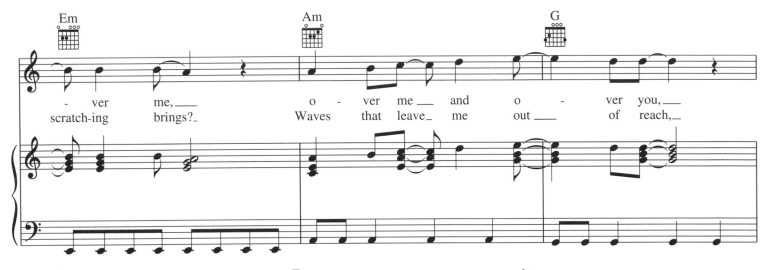

- ver me, ___ o - ver me ___ and o - ver you, ___
scratch-ing brings? ___ Waves that leave ___ me out ___ of reach, ___

stuck to - geth - er with ___ God's glue. ___ It's gon - na get ___ stick - i -
break - ing on ___ your back like a beach... Will we ev - er live

er, ___ too... It's been a long, hot ___ sum - mer. ___ Let's get
in peace? 'cause those that ___ can't do ___
left it ___ in the ___

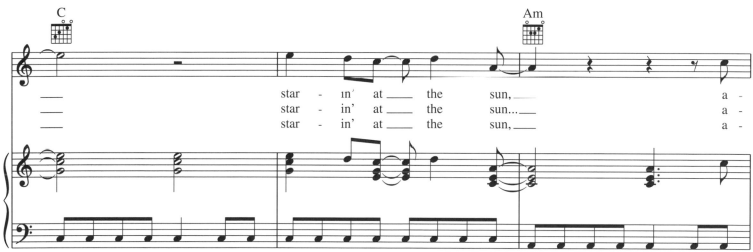

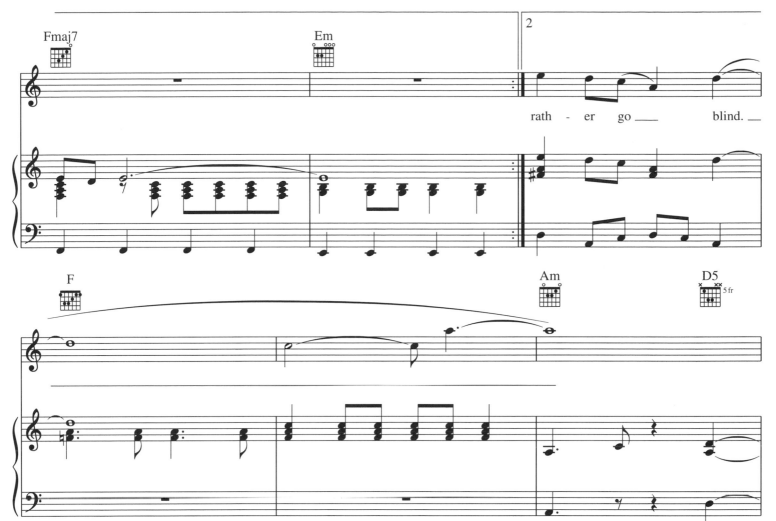

rath - er go ___ blind. ___

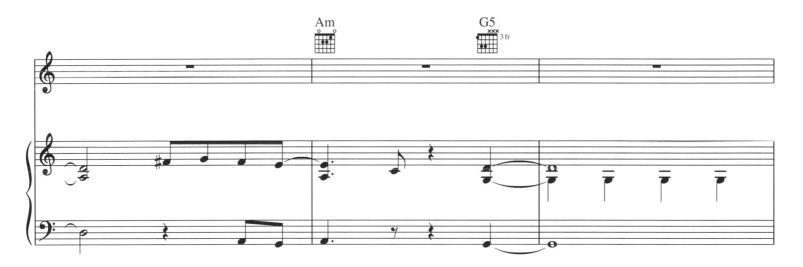

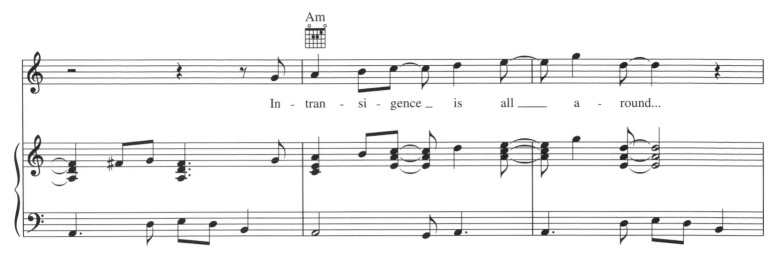

In - tran - si - gence __ is all __ a - round...

Mil - i - tar - y still __ in town, __ ar - mour plat - ed

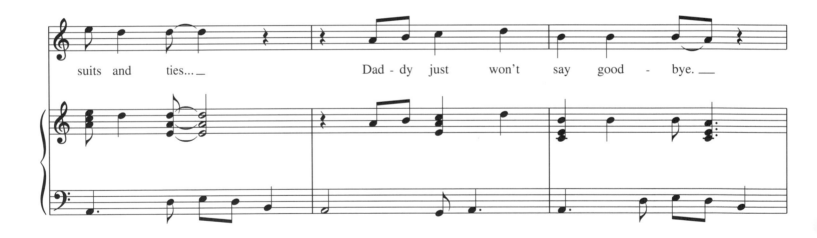

suits and ties... __ Dad - dy just won't say good - bye. __

Ref - er - ee __ won't blow __ the whis - tle. God is good, but

D.S. al Coda

will HE lis - ten? I'm near - ly great, but there's __ some-thing I'm miss - ing. I

CODA

hap - py to _____ go blind. _____

(Vocal 1st time only)

Repeat and Fade

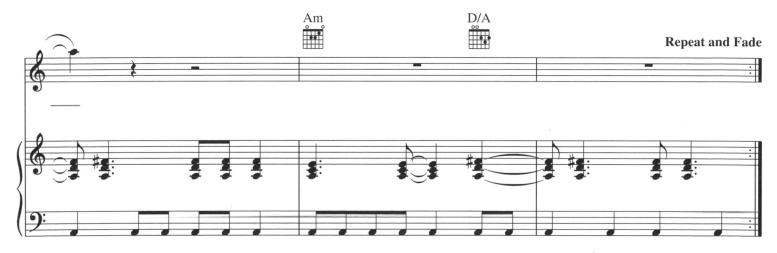

NUMB

Lyrics by BONO and THE EDGE
Music by U2

120

numb.) __   (I   feel __   numb.) _

Additional Lyrics

5. Don't breathe, hold me tight, don't panic, it's
Not that bad; just try and win.
Don't change your brand, don't listen to the band,
Don't ape, don't gape, don't change your shape.
Have another grape.

6. Don't plead, don't bridle, don't shackle, don't grind,
Don't curve don't swerve, lie, die, serve.

Don't theorize, realize, polarise, glance, dance,
Dismiss, apologize.

Don't spy, don't lie, don't try, imply, detain, explain,
Start again.

Don't triumph, don't coax, don't cling, don't hoax, don't
Freak, peak, don't leak, don't speak.

7. Don't project, don't connect, protect,
Don't expect, suggest.

Don't project, don't connect, protect,
Don't expect, suggest.

8. Don't struggle, don't jerk, don't collar, don't work, don't
Wish, don't fish, don't teach, don't reach,

Don't borrow, don't break, don't fence, don't steal, don't
Pass, don't press, don't try, don't feel.

9. Don't touch, don't dive, don't suffer, don't rhyme, don't
Fantasize, don't rise, don't lie.

Don't project, don't connect, protect,
Don't expect, suggest.

Don't project, don't connect, protect,
Don't expect, suggest.

THE FIRST TIME

Lyrics by BONO and THE EDGE
Music by U2

Moderately

mp

I have a lov- er,
I have a broth- er

a lov- er like no oth- er.
when I'm a broth- er in need.

She got soul, soul, soul, sweet soul, ___
I spend my whole time run- ning; _____

124

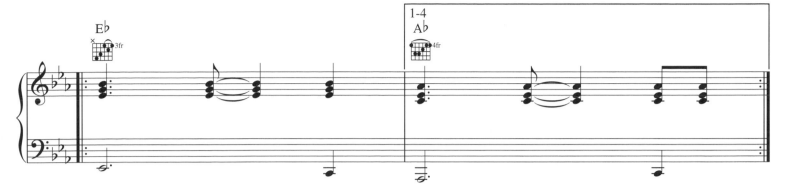

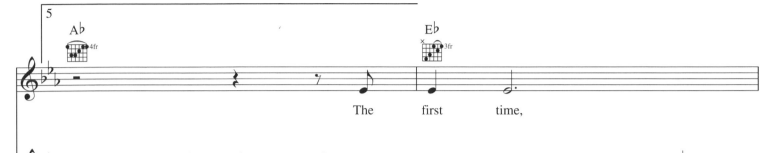

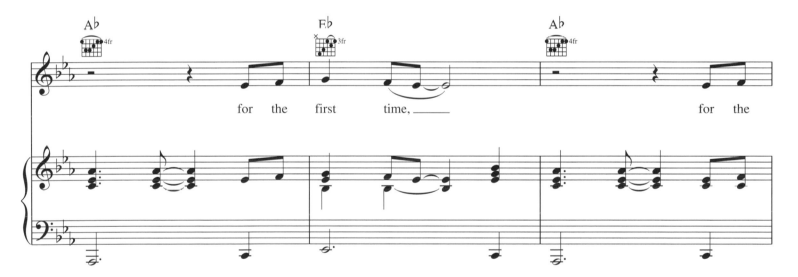

The first time,

for the first time, _____ for the

first time I feel love.

THE FLY

Lyrics by BONO and THE EDGE
Music by U2

Moderately fast

N.C.

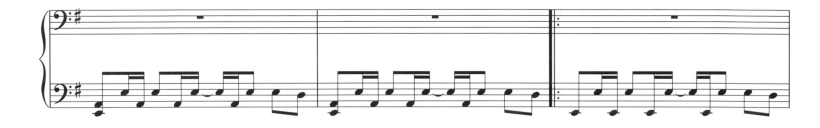

(Spoken:) Oh, baby child,   *(Sung:)* It's   no

se - cret that the stars __ are fall - ing from __ the sky. __ It's no

se - cret that our world __ is in dark - ness to - night. They say the

sun is some - times __ e - clipsed by a moon. __ You know I don't

see you when she walks in the room. It's no

128

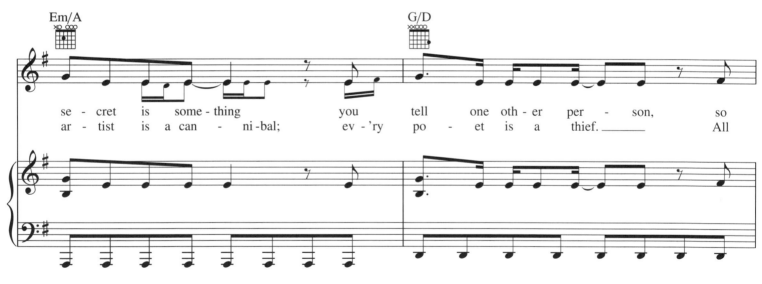

It's no

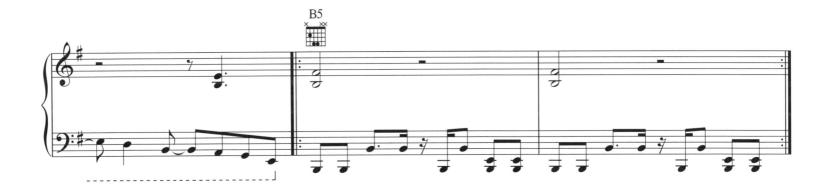

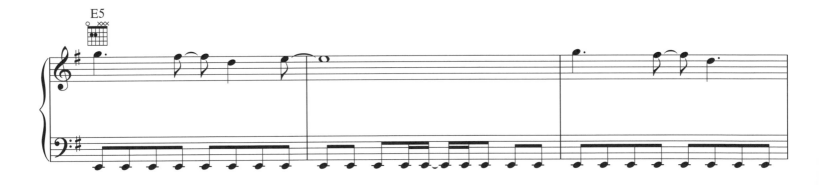

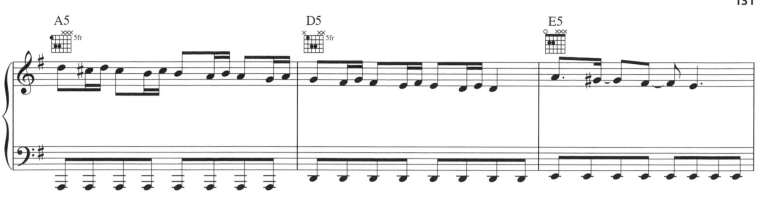

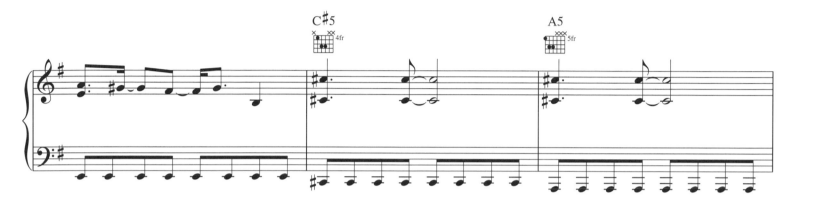

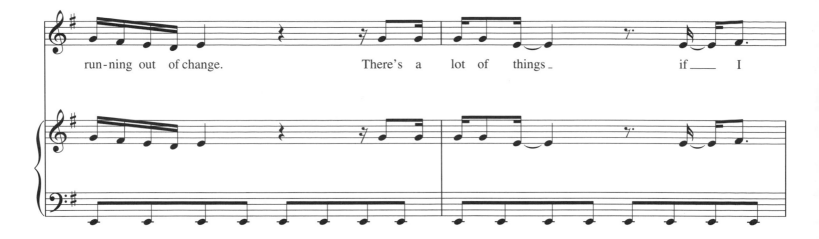

run-ning out of change. There's a lot of things _____ if _____ I

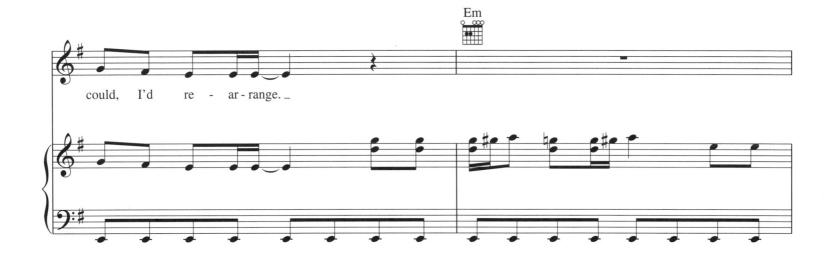

could, I'd re - ar - range. _____

rit.